BABER
FIRST OF THE MOGULS

BABER
FIRST OF THE MOGULS

BY

FERNAND GRENARD

Translated and adapted by
HOME WHITE & RICHARD GLAENZER

GYAN

Published by

Gyan Publishing House
5, Ansari Road
Daryaganj, New Delhi-110002
Phone: 011-47034999, 9811692060
E-mail: books@gyanbooks.com

Distribution Network
gyanbooks.com
India, USA, Canada, UK, Australia, France

ISBN : 978-81-212-6607-9 (PB)
First Published, 1930

2nd Impression 2021

Printed at: Gyan Press, Delhi.

Baber
First of the Moguls
Author: Fernand Grenard

BABER
FIRST OF THE MOGULS

By

FERNAND GRENARD

Translated and adapted by

HOME WHITE & RICHARD GLAENZER

Baber, the '*Panther*', Inspecting a garden. Page from a manuscript of the '*Baber Nameh*'. Miniature of the Mughal School. Last quarter of the 16th century. British Musuem, London.

CONTENTS

FOREWORD

WHEN, in 1876, Queen Victoria assumed the crown of the Empire of the Indias, she (or more likely, Disraeli) might have contended that socially the House of Hanover had at last arrived. For it was such a kingly holding as not even the most conservatively wild Hanoverian could have dared imagine three hundred years earlier. Vast in population and in wealth, vast in its lion's share of the world's area, it was vast also in tradition of a grandeur to beggar the antecedents of the English Victoria. The first Tudor Henry had in England only a second-rate European power, and Ernst of Brunswick-Hanover was a phlegmatic midge unknown beyond the obscure boundaries of his country when the Empire of India flamed up before the startled eyes of history. Created suddenly in one great piece within a breathless few years, settled deeply on its foundations, the dynasty of the Grand Moguls ruled over it without interruption until they perished of sheer inanition in 1862. Hanover might well be thought an interloper in this empire that has never ceased to exist, to which the passing of four hundred years has merely given fresh strength. It has changed officials and titles, but its framework, its body, is that given by its founder, Baber.

Infinitely less known than his ancestor Tamerlane, Baber has taken the prize away from that terrifying conqueror in point of grandeur and permanence of work accomplished. Even further: exclude his generalship, his political genius, his genius for organization; the man himself is worth more than his bizarre forebear.

His life is spun of the most extraordinary and various exploits, all of them touched by the immediate personality of the man, and hence romantic. Heir to a tiny principality in Turkestan, Farghana, he threw it away in wild adventures of his youth, and was left completely stripped and dispossessed, drawing out a miserable life in the exile of vagabondage—after the manner of Eastern potentates. Suddenly he emerged, king, as by a miracle, of Kabul. He spent twenty years in confirming his position in Afghanistan, in regaining the Central Asian empire of Tamerlane, and finally in conquering within a few months the half of Hindustan. With a vigorous and alert pen he set down the circumstantial history of those prodigious affairs, so that we are permitted to look upon a rare thing: the intimate character and motives of an Asiatic prince, a contemporary of our Renaissance... Baber is worth writing about, is worth reading about, because he combines an incessant activity in war and an astonishing personal vigour with a profound cultivation of mind and a sympathetic gaiety. His are qualities that win our hearts as they won those of his companions in arms.

To divest this engaging conqueror of the half-shadow that obscures him, we need only put his memoirs before a lay public. No historiographer's skill is needed to understand such a man. We shall permit ourselves, here and there, merely to add our more particular knowledge of Asiatic countries, gained from travel . . . a significant knowledge, we think, since time is motionless in the Orient. What Baber saw we may see. And out of the pages of the man's own book every instant rise those same fresh and distinct images, which will, we hope, communicate something of their own vitality to the pages that follow.

FERNAND GRENARD.

BABER

First of the Moguls

CHAPTER ONE

THE PANTHER CUB

A PERFECT drama is hard to come by. Imperfection seems to be the laws of the theatre. The first act of a play will be excellently done ; and after that the piece will die on its feet. Or after an inadequate beginning the final acts will roar colossally by, like a giant without a head. There will be climax without suspense, or there will be suspense without its climax. Characters will boggle at the slightest of difficulties and then knock the biggest down without starting so much as a single bead of perspiration. Logic and reason will appear and vanish as inconsequently as a butterfly.

Of all the playwrights, the one formerly called the Muse of History is perhaps the worst offender. Rarely does she conceive a play perfect in all of its details. Only rarely does she design perfect sets for all of her acts. And most rarely does she find a perfect actor for the leading part. But when she succeeds, as she occasionally does, the world applauds for centuries.

The scene is India. The plot is world-conquest. The actor is Baber, Panther of Farghana, Tiger of India, creator of an immense empire, and First of the Moguls.

The curtain rises upon a perfect drama.

The prelude is artful in its apparent obscurity and unimportance : it is laid at Akhsai, a little fortified town of Farghana that lay within its encircling walls on the height of a great clay cliff whose base was worn by the cold waters of the Kassan. In the Year of the Hegira 899, on Monday, the fourth day of Ramadan—that is to say, on the ninth of June in the year 1494 of our reckoning—the ruler of Farghana, Omar Sheik Mirza, direct in blood from Tamerlane, a man thirty-eight years of age, his face ruddy and lightly bearded, short of stature, and so wide of waist that his clothes were constantly splitting under the strain, mounted to his dovecote that was perched at the very summit of the cliff.

He was a robust and valiant warrior, a joyous drinker and a generous one, a lover of poetry and backgammon. But he had too much ambition, and it had just put him in very evil case. His entire reign, up to that moment, had been spent in vain intrigues and useless warfare against his eldest brother, Sultan Ahmed. For he aspired to replace him on the more glorious throne of Samarkand. But he had succeeded only in bringing against himself that prince and another neighbour of his, the Khan of the Jagatai Mongols, whose sister Sheik Mirza had married. Both of these men were anxious to put away such a turbulent relative.

Both were marching upon him, the Sultan from Samarkand, and the Khan from Tashkent. Sheik Mirza had mounted to his dovecote to watch for their unwelcome approach.

The structure gave way beneath his weight. Sheik

Mirza whirled into the ravine below and made way instantly for his successor, the governor of Andijan.

Thus abruptly the Sheik left his little kingdom to his son the governor. When, the day after the event, a messenger galloped into Andijan, the capital, sought out the heir in his summer palace, told him his news, and bade him come at once to Akhsai, it was an eleven-year-old boy who leaped into the saddle and rode to take possession of the crown—king at this perilous juncture.

At his birth, one of the *khojas*, those pious people who lavished their spiritual counsels on the Mussulman princes of the day, had given him the Arab name, Zahir-ud-Din Muhammad, which signified Defender of the Faith. But the family and the chieftains, finding this too long to manage, called him Baber, which in Turkish meant Panther. It was an old family name, destined to make a great noise in the world. His Indian foes interpreted it correctly when they translated the name as Tiger.

The situation was grave, almost without hope, in the face of such formidable adversaries as the two allied sovereigns. Sultan Ahmed from Samarkand had already occupied Uratepe, Khojent and Marghelan. The Mongol relative, Mahmud Khan, was about to lay siege to Akhsai.

But suddenly ill luck befell them Sultan Ahmed lost too many cattle in the swamps of a certain river, and an epidemic notably thinned out the number of his horses. When he arrived before Baber's capital, he was too weak and discouraged to do anything but make peace with the followers of his nephew. He departed for Samarkand, and died *en route*. As for the Mongolian uncle, Mahmud Khan, he too fell sick and departed.

It was more from tribal jealousy than from hope of great gain that Baber's relatives had visited him. His Farghana is a small country lying in the middle valley of the Syr river at the foot of the high mountains whose passes lead to Kashgar and to China—a small country lodged in the heart of Asia. Set in the midst of massive snow peaks, its plateaux are barren of anything save rock, pine and pasture-land, rather poor in grass. Along its river bed it sprawls widely in shale, sand and marsh.

Mongols and Turks had invaded it lately. But before their coming, its inhabitants had fought the inhospitable country with reservoirs and irrigating canals. These had created fertile oases : Osh, Asfara, extensive Andijan and Marghelan, Khokan, Khojent, Akhsai and Kassan.

These oases are magnificent parks of elm, poplar and willow that shade the running streams and cover the roads, dusty now under the gallop of horses, the clicking hoofs of asses and the furtive tread of camels. The beasts are gaudy in their trappings ; vivid and bizarre colours glow upon the men, the women and the children, bespeaking them for what they are : merchants, artisans, farmers, going to the great markets of the country.

Suddenly the crowd melts away ; it forms rank by the side of the road. Talking ceases. A distant noise has disturbed them : over and down a hill and through a high gate set in the walls of masonry sweeps a body of horsemen, clearing the way before them with a great rattle of swords, bows and quivers banging on mail and stirrup. A nobleman is setting out to serve in the wars.

He is a Turk or Mongol, whose ancestors were shepherds wandering over the steppes and mountains to the north. Time out of mind they have descended upon the quiet villages in the midst of their cultivated valleys, for pillage and for ransom. They have ended by living among the villagers, always reserving to themselves the business of fighting, the only trade they or their sons have ever understood. The military and political functions are in their hands alone. It is their reward for competent usurpation. Thus, this particular overlord is no more than exercising his privilege this morning.

The native population, however much it may appear to the contrary, are not lazy or cowardly. They have simply found that it is better investment to pay for their immunity. They are too busy in field, shop and workroom to waste time at sword-play. One cannot go rushing away to cleave an enemy's skull just when the iron is red-hot in the forge or when trade is brisk at the bazaar and labour needful at the ripe harvest. It is better to submit to extortion ; better, since the toll is inevitable, to pay without fighting than to fight and then pay . . . Oh, doubtless the system has its inconveniences. The Turkish lord sweats at his troublesome industry only too willingly, sometimes to satisfy ambition, sometimes for gain, sometimes merely for amusement. As a result the population suffers under requisition, rapine and violence from every quarter of the wind. But it can usually dodge the heavier blows ; and though the storms may be frequent, they never last long.

So, patiently sheltering themselves as best they can, the people maintain and develop their civilization through many, many years. They thrive in spite of the desert marauders, and in defiance of them. They do more: little by little they win over the troopers ; they captivate them, teach them to play with arts that preserve and sweeten life. At the peroid of which we speak, the greater part of the turbulent nobles are lulling their fierce hearts with the harmonies of Persian music and poetry ; they are being enchanted by the pure curves traced by architects from Iran, by the delicate colours of the painters of miniatures and the glazers of poetry, by the subtle undulations of the calligraphers. They are demanding of the craftsmen at the bazaars sumptuous fabrics, more work in enamel, in inlaid bronze, in damascened arms. And golden inscriptions on sword blades are a warrior's confession of his unconscious surrender to luxurious Peace.

To be sure, Farghana as a seat of the arts was not comparable, even remotely, with Samarkand or Herat. It was on the edge of the civilized world, on the borders of nomadic savagery. But at least it abundantly produced all the materials for a leisured living—cattle on the hills, grain in the broad fields, a profusion of excellent fruits: apricots, strawberries, almonds, pomegranates. The melons there were so delicious that when, after long years in India, Baber recalled the memory of them, his heart-strings were touched, and the conqueror wept. In the height of the season the gardeners gave them away to any who asked.

But the attractions of that province were not such as could content the mighty heart that was soon to bestir itself within the rocky borders of the place. Nor were they sufficient as resources to make possible any considerable extension of those borders. If wisely spent, the revenues of Farghana could maintain three or four thousand soldiers; a conqueror must have a hundred times as many. For his support in war he has need of a giant state ; but Farghana was only a weak child separated from the mother-empire whose bounds the Emir Tamerlane had stretched from China to the Ægean Sea and from Delhi to the Muscovite borders.

Tamerlane no more than Genghis Khan, Charlemagne or Clovis, had dreamed of an empire firm in part and whole like the meshes of a vast net. At his death he deliberately broke up and distributed his realm. And the loose fragments had given no clue to builders of empire that might follow. His emipre had been held together by the sword ; at best, the State was its scabbard. A sword severs, it does not unite. And the sons of Timur repeated the blunder of their father.

There was an exception : Shah Rukh, fourth and last to survive of the sons. He ruled over all of the patrimony save Asia Minor and Syria. Generous and humane, he was able and fortunate in his wars, which he waged only to preserve the integrity of the empire. The forty-two years of his reign slipped by in comparative peace. And he left behind him the memory of an administration that was firm and just, a prosperity that was most uncommon, an unheard-of development of internal commerce and of foreign relations with China and India, Egypt and Byzantium. Protector of arts and sciences, himself a scholar, founder of a rare library at his palace in Herat, he presided over one of the most brilliant periods of Persian civilization. His historian called him Khakan-i-Saïd, the Fortunate King.

His son was his successor. But Ulugh Beg never grew to the ample garments of his father. He was, nevertheless, a man remarkable for heart and intelligence, able poet, erudite theologian, eminent mathematician. He was the sun of a flashing galaxy of philosophers, writers and artists. He adorned Samarkand with monuments. He built there an observatory where he produced his astronomical tables, superior in exactness to any previously made.

But in studying the order of the stars, Ulugh Beg overlooked the disorder of humanity ; too assiduously occupied with poetry, he ignored the sinfulness of mankind. The reins wavered in his exquisite hands, and in 1449, his own son, a poet like himself, had him put to death.

From that point on, the confused course of Timur's empire becomes wearisome to follow : father and son, uncle and nephew, brother and cousin, husband and wife, mother and child, vassal and suzerain were whirled about in the most extraordinary confusion of revolts, betrayals, secret coalitions, marriages, harem intrigues, imprisonments, exiles, blindings, poniardings, poisonings. Family affairs turned toward crime as naturally as a tiger kills for food—except that here one of the same blood was apparently ordained by nature to be the killer. The Timurids would seem to have been a breed of murderous monsters.

But on closer view these people turn out to be men, very simple men who followed scrupulously the given rules of the game. In settling their arguments concisely by force and treachery, they employed methods approved by their age. These rivalries of theirs, instead of pitting city against city, state against state, nation against nation, were confined in the most natural way in the world to the family, the reigning family.

The period was a bewildering paradox: rich in magnanimous ruffians, men who could not endure dictation, yet were merciful to a fault when not driven; men who were an incredible opposite when mercy was expected of them. Their cruelty and knavery frequently overleaped the generous limits of the times; and those limits are in themselves hard to define. For example: Baber Mirza,* grandson of Shah Rukh, signed a treaty of peace with his brother Muhammad. The latter perjured himself, recommenced fighting, and was defeated and captured. His brother reproached him for his disloyalty. "It was the only price to pay for a crown," was his answer. He happened to be wrong that time, for what he had purchased was death.

This Muhammad and his generation were contem-

* Mirza is not a proper name but a Persian title. Placed before a name it denotes a scholar; after a name, a prince. It is a contraction of Emir Zadeh, the son of an emir.

poraries of Machiavelli. The Florentine would not have felt out of place among them. And yet these descendants of Tamerlane whose miserable quarrels need not burden the memory were not wholly without their points. Many of them were debauchees of the most degraded type, but all were vigorous, brave in combat, stoical under pain; some were generous; the majority, devoted to pleasures of the mind. Occasionally, one was found who had no taste for blood: he would take refuge in asceticism, in mysticism. Others gave themselves to study and to the arts. For instance, Ghyas-ud-Din Baisonkor, son of Shah Rukh, retired to practise his talent as calligraphist; around him he gathered some forty artists who produced marvels some of which may be seen in Constantinople to this day.

After Ulugh Beg, Abu-Saïd, grandfather of Baber, brought once more under central authority most of Shah Rukh's domain. But at his death the disintegration became complete and permanent. His eldest son, Ahmed, enjoyed Samarkand and Bokhara; his second had Badakshan and the wild country between the Hissar Mountains and the Hindu-Kush; another son, Kabul and Ghazni. The father of Baber had to be content with Farghana.

And finally the Sultan Hussayn Baikara, the most puissant of all these kings, possessed himself of Khorassan and the neighbouring countries. Like many a man of the period, Hussayn had, quite involuntarily, acquired a taste for adventure. Three times forced to fly for his life into the steppes, three times he returned with a handful of men; and the third time spelled triumph. He re-illumined Shah Rukh's capital and made it synonymous with his own splendour. His pen was nearly as mighty as his sword. He sustained a vigorous correspondence with Jami, the great poet of the century, who honoured the court with his presence. The death of the poet was made the occasion of public mourning. The sovereign himself was a pall-bearer, the funeral oration was delivered by the chief minister, Mir-Ali-Shir, historian, theologian, statesman of singular authority, and most illustrious of Turkish poets. It was another Augustan era, in line with Timur's dream. But Hussayn Baikara was no Timur as his later years and his end will disclose.

Farghana was not glorious. At the moment, it had but one claim to distinction above the other kingdoms: it was thoroughly exposed to attacks from nomads of the steppes. Its luckless function was to protect the other states from such attacks. In front of it spread the land of the Mongol Khans, descendants of Jagatai, second son of Genghis Khan. This was now divided, like a more classic realm, into three parts and held by relatives who furnished one another with an enemy—when itching for a fight. In addition to these, Kipchak, between Tashkent and the Urals, was held by the Kazaks, a confederation of Turks that exists at the present day. And, finally, as the last of Farghana's busy neighbours, there was the main body of the Uzbek Turks, temporarily on bad terms with fractions of themselves, but ready to reunite against Baber.

Such was the political and racial nucleus of circumstance that was destined to produce the future conqueror—Baber. Such was the complexity out of which the man created a power as simple as it was almost supreme. Far from losing heart because of its smallness as a cornerstone, he felt that he had been marked with the seal of destiny. "The divine favour," he wrote in his Memoirs, "has always directed my affairs in the most agreeable and fortunate manner."

It was this divine favour that led him to erect, far from the place of his birth, one of the famous empires of the earth. But before he achieved his destiny he was to undergo the most astonishing vicissitudes. He must fall, after successes that were as ephemeral as they were striking, into the lowest depths of the forsaken and the miserable.

He endured all his misfortunes without despairing. After each catastrophe he set out with a whole heart and good humour to regain the highway, Fortune's highway, to which he felt he would hold in due course.

Baber's serene faith in his manifest destiny is no legend planted by the flattery of his scribes and nourished by his successors, nor is it the glib attribution of more recent historians. It pervades his Memoirs. It cannot be ignored.

CHAPTER TWO

SAMARKAND WON AND LOST

FULLY to comprehend Baber's prodigious destiny, one must be reminded of the political state of the country. Asia was split up into a great number of kingdoms, some of them powerful enough, but all of them equally unstable. And for a good reason: the law of succession was as confusing as the smoke from the fisherman's vessel of copper, the smoke that resolved itself into a malevolent jinn. All the sons of a ruler, all of his descendants, no matter how remote their relation, considered themselves vested with equal and entire authority; inheritance was nearly a figure of speech.

As a further complication, the princes depended upon a military nobility, the members of which were attached to one or another by personal volition and sentiments of fidelity. The duty of homage, already fragile enough in European feudalism, was infinitely more so in Asia, where the lordship was not established upon the land, and where power was not inherent in its organization. A lord would pass from one fief to another as circumstances blew him: he changed sovereigns, as they fell this way and that in their quarrels, hardly less often than he changed his linen.

Thus with Baber, too. Before he can accomplish his destiny, he must fight his relatives, his own nobles, his own soldiers. Less favoured than some, he must even lose his heritage, and be turned out-of-doors as an adventurer. But when with empty hands he begins his wandering, he will carry at his saddle-bow certain unimpeachable rights. In his veins runs the blood of great empire-builders, of Timur and of Genghis Khan. He will recruit new fidelities on the way.

Turkish and Mongol by this inheritance, Baber had the best of the barbaric traits and the best of the civilized. In appearance he retained few of the former. His portrait is that of a man with finely drawn features, a long face and a well-cut nose, a slight beard coming to a point on his chin, a short moustache that lends value to the delicate irony of his smile. The Mongol shows in the narrow slits of his eyes. But those rovers of the desert left him characteristics far more valuable, virtues of capital importance to a political career : independence and stubbornness. When ill winds blew, he took them head on. He could remain alone yet firm against every man and thing, without repining ; watch persistently for that great wave which would bear him up to his star.

He had need of every possible material and spiritual aid. Though no longer menaced by the two uncles, he had always internal disorder to disquiet him. One doubts that he could have weathered through except for his grandmother. Aisan-Daulat was her name, a woman of unusually shrewd intelligence and common sense. She employed her qualities in exploits that would have delighted the heart of Brantôme.

Twelve years before, her husband Yunas, Khan of the Jagatai Mongols, had been defeated in battle by some of his relations. He had sought to reprovision his army at Tashkent, which then belonged to Sultan Ahmed, his son-in-law. His chieftains, having little liking for him, abandoned him on the spot and went over to the governor in a body. Aided by them, the official captured Yunas and Aisan-Daulat and held them prisoners. She being counted a prize of war, was handed over to one of the state officers, a man of some distinction. The wedding night came, the new spouse presented himself before his new princess, who apparently was diposed to look kindly upon him. But after he had entered her bedchamber, she made a sign to her maids : they locked the doors, threw themselves upon the bridegroom and stabbed him to death. At dawn his corpse was pushed out of the door. The governor demanded an explanation. Aisan-Daulat gave one : "My husband is Yunas Khan. You presumed to give me to another. I have killed him. You may do the same with me if you like." Struck with admiration, Sultan Ahmed returned her to her husband.

Obviously, she was the woman to protect her grandson Baber against the innumerable intrigues hatched about him. Sultan Mahmud, another uncle, Prince of Hissar and successor at Samarkand of his brother Ahmed, was busy trying to despoil his nephew, and for that purpose had entered into a conspiracy with the major-domo of Baber's palace. Unfortunately for the Sultan, the major-domo excelled at archery, mall, and leapfrog, and at nothing else. So one day, while he was at the chase, Aisan-Daulat profited by his absence to dispose of his fellow-conspirators.

He himself continued on the chase, though with greater dispatch than before, and toward Samarkand. But, overtaken in the middle of the night by soldiers sent in pursuit of him, he died on the point of an arrow.

The picture presented by the prince seems to be that of a lamb in a field of snow, surrounded by wolves with notably large red mouths. Yet here and there his troubles were lightened and his position made more secure. His nobles were diligent in his behalf. They repelled an invasion of Abou-Bekr, who had meant to try his luck in Farghana. One of their own number in Asfara, who had dared to proclaim the sovereignty of the king of Samarkand, they brought to terms by a siege. They retook Khojent, thereby restoring the kingdom to its former unity. They failed only once, against Uratepe, which fell into the designing hands of the uncle from Tashkent.

But Baber could do more than win mere victories in the field. He showed ability of a subtler kind when he paid court to his Mongol uncle, Mahmud Khan, the enemy of yesterday. The Khan received him seated beneath a beautiful canopy in the centre of a garden. Baber was presented in the fashion prescribed by Genghis Khan for the reception of princes. He entered the garden alone, he knelt thrice at the far end of the carpeted path ; he advanced ; the Khan rose to honour his guest, to embrace him ; the lad returned to his place and knelt yet again. And the uncle, fairly enchanted by so courteous a nephew, gave him a free hand in the events about to follow.

Sultan Mahmud of Samarkand, another uncle not to be confused with the preceding, died but a few months after his accession. His younger son, Baisonkor, only eighteen years of age, was the only one present at his demise. The people accepted this fact as reason enough for letting him fill the empty throne. This he did with honour for a time, putting to rout the Mongol Khan, who was coming in too great haste to have his bite at this defenceless morsel, Samarkand. But he committed the imprudence of favouring strangers about him, giving offence to the family of the Tarkhans, high lords of Samarkand and Bokhara. These withdrew and sought out Ali Mirza, third son of the dead ruler; they proclaimed him Padishah, and returned to surround Baisonkor in the citadel. The latter retired to a private room to reflect upon their terms, and while the nobles guarded the front door, he escaped by the rear, ran across the courtyard, scaled the walls, escaped from the city by a subterranean passage, and found refuge in the cave of a *khoja* of one of his friends.

These *khojas* could impress such superstitious Mussulmans as the Turks. They were a religious sect who performed pseudo-miracles, mysteriously punished offenders, and were, in short, fully as redoubtable as the old magicians of the primitive forests. By consequence, no one dared violate the sanctuary of Baisonkor. This retirement did not last long; his partisans, who included most of the population, induced him to return. Ali Mirza was besieged in the fortress and made prisoner there. His captors held red-hot irons before his eyes in order to blind him;

but the operation was unsuccessful. Ali Mirza, however, did not let that fact appear, so he also was allowed to retire to the cave of a *khoja*. From there he went to Bokhara, where, his brother pursuing him, he managed to defeat him, thanks to the help of the Tarkhans.

Informed of these various excursions, Baber took horse and rode toward Samarkand, in the last days of June (1496). He was not yet fourteen years old, a tender age at which to have formed such a resolution by himself. In his Memoirs he never dwells upon his personal achievements, never boasts of his shrewdness and initiative. In serious conjunctures he always consulted with his generals, and his plan was not always the one to be approved. On this occasion he limits himself to the remark that he went merely to assert his rights. The argument is not too convincing, since, as we have seen, every one else had *his* rights too. Probably there was very little debate, for under Omar Sheik Mirza his lords had become accustomed to storming Samarkand upon any and all occasions, being happy in a fight, with as much disdain for defeat as they had little fear. In addition, of course, Baber was, like all the other pretenders, grandson of Abu-Saïd. It was irrelevant that he was the issue of a younger son.

Another competitor was added to the struggle for Samarkand in the person of Masoud, Prince of Hissar. As the eldest son of Sultan Mahmud, his claims would seem to have been paramount.

The three armies converged upon the ancient capital of Tamerlane. There was four months of mild fighting that led nowhere. Then Ali Mirza proposed an interview with his cousin Baber. Their armies drew up along the river at Samarkand, one on the left, the other on the right bank, out of arrow-range of each other. Prudently the two cousins drew near each other, accompanied by four or five horsemen. Talking from their horses, they agreed to join forces the following spring and occupy Samarkand. The city would fall to Baber, the country around to his cousin.

In May, 1497, Baber began the new campaign with his ally. Soon the entire country—fortified towns, mountains and plains, everything except the capital—was in his hands. One little fact shows his sense of order and discipline, which was to be one of the reasons for his future success. Near his camp the natives had opened up a market for the convenience of the besiegers. One afternoon in a moment of forgetfulness Baber's men raided the stalls. The young prince announced that there was to be immediate and complete restitution of the plunder. Next morning not so much as an extra needle or bit of thread was to be found in the hands of the soldiers.

Meanwhile, the siege of Samarkand went forward. Those within the city attempted sorties, in one of which the citizens participated. The royal chronicler does not hesitate to record that several of the artisans were put to torture, because they were irregulars : they had long ago surrendered the right to bear arms, they had no permission to fight.

Winter did not freeze the fire of Baber's enthusiasm. He set up barracks of stone, of clay, of scantling and felt. His troops were sheltered. And at last, after six months of unremitting investment, the town, at the end of its resources, surrendered. Baisonkor fled with a few hundred of his half-starved supporters.

So, upon one of the most illustrious cities of Asia, equalled in splendour and dignity only by Herat ; upon the roof of the Azure Palace that Tamerlane had set above the citadel ; upon that great warrior's mausoleum whose incomparable dome was banded with gigantic inscriptions ; upon mosques and colleges with their majestic portals ornamented with enamelled brick where the night-blue of lapis blended with the day-blue of turquoise ; upon the *Mokatta* shrine, wrought in wood, carved and coloured after the manner of the Chinese ; upon the baths of Mirza and the observatory of Ulugh-Beg ; upon the Pavilion of Forty Columns and the Porcelain Tower brought from Cathay, symbols of greatness as well as marvels of art; upon the bazaars spread at their feet, hives of movement and business and wealth, where every guild produced its most superb work, where might be brought the finest paper, the rarest velvets—upon all of this magnificence now rested, possessively, the hand of a boy of fourteen. The world, he must have thought, had been made for the young.

The prince's position seemed pleasant enough, but he was learning that fortune is something of a butterfly, never sipping long at one flower. For example, it was far easier to play the role of victor or even that of vanquished—for Baisonkor had found comfortable quarters with Khosrau Khan at Kunduz—than it was to be paymaster. Baber could not transmute porcelain towers into silver. And he would have given mounds of glazed brick for a moderate payroll. He had no money for his men ! All the towns of the country had surrendered at the very first summons. Consequently, he could not decently plunder them for the booty with which he generally defrayed expenses. And the capital had been exhausted of the necessities of life during the siege ; the farmers of the suburbs even had to be furnished with seed. Monuments, works of art and martial glory are a lean diet. The warriors soon had enough of them ; they deserted in numbers until the prince had left in his army only a thousand men.

The state of things came to the ear of Uzzun Hassan, governor of Akhsai, the principal fortress of Farghana. In his opinion, certain fruits were rotten-ripe. He called in the deserters and with them besieged Andijan. A member of the clan of the mother of Jahangir, Baber's younger brother, he took the part of the junior on the theory that Baber owed him a share of his conquests or an equivalent.

Baber's mother and grandmother, shut up within Akhsai, sent out letter after letter, imploring him to come to their rescue. But that prince was busy taking nourishment from a bit of cotton moistened with broth. He was ill, so ill that he could not even speak. And, one night in March of 1498, a closed litter slipped inconspicuously out of Samarkánd with a pale, wasted lad in it who, one hundred days before, had entered the same gate to the clash of cymbals and the clatter of ten thousand horses, arrayed in yellow silks and regal velvets, a jewelled scimitar before him, lord of

Samarkand. Baber was not well, but he was well enough to exercise discretion and flee.

A week after, he arrived at Khojent only to learn that the governor of Andijan, despairing of the health of his master, had rendered up the place. He now besought help of his Mongol uncle from Tashkent. This politician marched forth to his aid and might have lent it had not the rebels blunted his spears with silver. As it was, he turned back. Abandoned by those men whose wives had been taken at Andijan, giving up the town as completely lost, supported by a mere two or three hundred faithful retainers "as good as they were powerless" ; stripped both of his heritage and of his conquests, the young prince wept. Even then he had not learned all there was to know about his uncle. Twice more was he to call upon the Khan of Tashkent, an old fox whose tastes ran more to plunder than to bloodshed ; and twice more was he to return to Khojent, defeated in all his plans and immediate hopes.

"Nevertheless," he writes in his Memoirs, "tormented as I was by the desire to reign and by the ambition to conquer, I could not bring myself to remain a spectator of events simply because of one or two checks." There shows the mainspring of his character: elastic and yet firm, and so regulated that when he fell he always landed on his feet.

Now Khojent was a miserable little town, an inferior oasis, incapable of supporting for very long a prince and two hundred and fifty fighting men with the long, sharp teeth of hunger ; so Baber, an unlucky gambler in need of a stake, asked a maternal uncle of his,

Muhammad Hussayn, to lend him the village of Beshaghir. This Muhammad Hussayn, father of the historian Mirza Muhammad Haidar, was of the family of the Doghlat, hereditary lords of Kashgar. He had been driven out by his cousin Abou-Bekr, but was still affluent. It was natural, therefore, that he should be in a position to aid his nephew, whose request he accordingly granted.

Soon the young prince installed himself in his borrowed town, and re-equipped his army. He then set out without loss of time toward Samarkand. He took Zamin in passing, and disregarding a fever from which he suffered at the time, hurried over the mountains to Rabat, hoping to surprise the place. He arrived early one dawn ; but he found the garrison warned and alert. Only seventy miles from Samarkand he was obliged to turn back.

Sultan Ali Mirza was in possession, having usurped the place of his cousin and former ally. He demanded that Baber should make peace, in other words, abandon his claims. Forced to submit, Baber found himself in an apparently hopeless dilemma, unable to go forward, and convinced that it was vain to return to Khojent, whose resources had been exhausted by his previous halt there. He camped for a few days in the high pastures on the side of the mountains, overwhelmed with anxiety and despair.

One day the usual devout *khoja* passed by the camp. Baber hailed him and asked him for advice. The man recited with imposing gravity the first *sura* of the Koran. The prince was deeply moved by the sacred words. And at that moment he saw a far-away horseman enter the little valley. It was an envoy of Ali Dost Tagai, the governor of Andijan, who had surrendered the place to Jahangir. He had come to beg forgiveness of Baber, to urge him to come to Marghelan, which he would give over into his hands. Baber looked upon the fellow as a traitor, as avaricious and insolent. Nevertheless, he did not hesitate. He left at once, rode night and day, stopping only to feed his horses.

At the end of the third night, having galloped one hundred and eighty miles, he was at the outskirts of the oasis of Marghelan. One of his counsellors then represented that the business was very risky, that it was the spider's invitation to a fly, that Ali Dost had given no sort of guarantee other than his own wretched word. "You would have done better to suggest that to me sooner," the prince replied sagely; "I cannot retreat now, with men and horses at the end of their endurance. Let God decide!" That again was Baber: prompt to seize a chance, rapid and resolute in executing a decision made and a fatalist once the die was cast.

At an early hour next morning he presented himself at the gates of the town, and found them closed. Ali Dost leaned through an embrasure in the walls and mentioned certain conditions; they were accepted. The gates were opened and Ali did homage to his lord. Besides his Mongol auxiliaries Baber had with him no more than two hundred men at arms. Half of these he sent east, half west, with instructions to gather an army, by force or persuasion. The bold gesture brought him an army, but not one that he dared to count on.

His adversaries seemed to have chosen their time well. Under Uzzun Hassan they hurried to Marghelan and began the reduction of it by famine. Being the debauched tyrants they were, however, they had not done wisely to come so far away from home ; by their excesses they had earned the hate of Farghana. Now that they were away, the people arose. Akhsai drove out its governor. Hassan immediately left his siege to retake the mutinous town. He was repulsed, and fell back upon Andijan, whose gates were at once shut in his face. Hassan was thus left in the embarrassing predicament of a rat whose holes are blocked while he is away foraging for cheese in a trap.

The cheering news came to Baber early one morning at Marghelan. He sprang into his saddle and covered the forty-eight miles to Andijan before nightfall. After an absence of fifteen months he was back again in his heritage, behind him a career already far more adventurous than many a hero of history or legend could boast.

Success did not lull him into carelessness. He forced Uzzun Hassan to capitulate and retire into Karateghin with a mere handful of his Mongol supporters. Most of them remained among their enemies in Farghana. They were harried by a stern vengeance. "These people," said the victorious chiefs, "have oppressed and pillaged our faithful vassals. They have ruined our best horses, they have paraded in our finest clothes, they have licked their chops over our mutton. We can recover some of that, perhaps, at the whipping-post." Baber thought that these complaints were legitimate. And he learned the lesson that policy and logic are two very different things, and that reason and justice are not always opportune. His three or four thousand Mongol auxiliaries, disturbed at seeing the lightning strike so near home, deserted to Jahangir, who still held Osh and Uzkent.

After a number of insignificant engagements, Baber fought what he termed his first regular battle against the allied forces of his brother and the insurgent Mongols. He defeated them, but the victory was not decisive. Despite his incessant activity, which even the ice of winter never halted, the military operations dragged on, complicated now by the hostile intervention of that interfering old fox, the uncle from Tashkent. Two of his barons, Ali Dost and Kanber Ali, a Mongol newcomer (who, according to Baber, talked too much and, as a consequence, badly), set themselves to arrange a peace between the two brothers. Being the most powerful of all the lords, they could impose their will upon the others and even upon Baber, as he found to his disgust. He gave in, and terms were arranged. The boundary of the two countries was to be the Syr river. Baber was to occupy the land to the south, Jahangir that to the north. And, this once agreed upon, the two brothers were able to unite their forces against Samarkand. In the event of success, the elder was to keep this latter country, and Farghana was to pass entirely into the hands of the younger.

Baber, meanwhile, upon reaching his seventeenth year, had found time to espouse Ayesheh, a cousin of his, after an engagement of twelve years' standing. He had found time; but the inclination had really been wanting. "If, even at the beginning, I had any affection for her," he says laconically, "it was never anything more than the sentiment of a husband for a wife." So great was his timidity toward her that only with the greatest difficulty could he bring himself to see her once every three weeks. It was scarcely enough. He had but one child by her, a daughter who died shortly after birth. After that, only his mother's insistence made him pay her a visit once every six months After that, she left him.

He was at an age when volatile emotions may easily take on the wrong colour in their escape. A beautiful young boy, son of a wandering merchant, was much more successful than Ayesheh. Bearing a name of good omen, Baberi, he inspired the young prince with a violent passion. The latter was so agitated in his presence, so overcome with feeling, that he dared not look at the boy or even speak to him. Without shoes or turban he wandered through the streets and gardens, forgetful of himself and of everything, mindful only of his passion, which he expressed in perfervid poems.

He was not always to be so indifferent to feminine graces, however.

My heart, now tangled in the black net of your hair,
Struggles no more, far from the torments of the world—

was written to a later love, and mistress, this time.

Furthermore, when he did meet the woman who pleased him, he proved capable of the most tender affection, the most touching solicitude, through many long years with her. We see him one day when his years were setting toward their grey decline, forgetting the glory of his majesty, running on foot ahead of that woman through a muddy street, clearing a way for her, with all the eagerness of a child, the devotion of a willing slave.

CHAPTER THREE

THEY WHO WIN SAMARKAND . . .

A MAN on the brink of a precipice could not have been more aware of the perils of his position than was Baber, marking time in Andijan. Ali Dost Tagai was a wolf thinly disguised as a lamb. If he had made himself agent of the reconciliation between Baber and his brother, he still had his appetite for fat, which the former might supply. So, for the moment, the wolf tried to play host to the panther cub. But, surly, old, hard-mouthed, he thoroughly disliked this royal stripling who was too enterprising to be easily led, too young to deserve command.

The hospitality of Ali Dost became distinctly Procrustean. He discharged the prince's faithful retainers, he robbed him of his friends, and despoiled those that were left. He was amazed at the prince's docility. Baber, it so happened, had looked about him hopelessly for some way out of his difficulties. His silence, therefore, was not of acquiescence but of pure discretion. He was biding his time.

He had need of self-control. Ali's son, Muhammad, had assumed kingly airs. He dressed in the finest scarlet cloth of Baghdad, held his own court and was lackeyed by innumerable retainers. Even a popinjay's money is power. Baber, beholding the begemmed Muhammad, looked at his own modest garments and said nothing. He refused to be baited. As for being eclipsed by a coxcomb, time would tell.

And now came word that a certain fine warrior, Sultan Ahmed Tanbal, the chief of Baber's brother's adherents, had joined hands with Ali Dost with no friendly intent toward the prince. The latter knew that the coalition was of considerable strength and deemed it politic to overlook its existence. Few men twice his age would have faced with such fortitude and sagacity so humiliating a position.

On the face of it, the reason for the whole curious state of affairs is not altogether clear. But at least it has its understandable side, given a social system whose ruler was nothing more than the titular head of a loose confederacy of independent nobles, and whose term of office depended upon the fiery whims of warriors with infinitely various appetites. A hundred centres of authority flourished about him, all theoretically equal. He was no more conspicuous than a royal oakling in a forest of oaks.

Among the Mongols, the organism of the State that grew out of the ancient classical city did not exist. In the Roman world the senators were everything when they acted as a body and nothing when they acted individually; but in the Asiatic world the nobles would not submit to the unified flexibility of that idea. They would have called it slavery, if a prince had been so ill-advised as to suggest such a thing. Everyone worked by and for himself; and to the chief he owed no faith save that prompted by friendship, personal advantage, or the traditions of his family.

Allegiance, in short, was not explicit. Had it been, it would have frightened such individualists, they being too much accustomed to their time-honoured game of infidelities.

Before very long, Ali Mirza was refreshing his memory of that characteristic. He was soon wearing as tight a pair of shoes in Samarkand as did Baber in Andijan. And he owed them to the lords of the powerful Tarkhan family, who claimed practically all of the revenues of his state and left him scarcely enough for the essential crust and clout. While they spent his money with superb munificence, buying homage, building palaces, scattering jewels in the streets—one of them maintaining six thousand retainers and seven hundred hunting falcons—Sultan Ali carried about a crown of brass and an empty belly.

So it came about that he conspired to rid himself of such expensive and dangerous vassals. He elected the sword as his instrument of negotiation, and called first on the Mongols of Tashkent, then on Baber, to help him in Samarkand.

The young prince hastily patched up a specious reconciliation with his adversaries and, before they could stop him, was in his saddle. He had made camp but twice when he learned that behind his back his enemies were about to take Osh from him, and that the rest of his domain was similarly threatened. But he shrugged his shoulders and rode forward, disdaining to defend such a rattletrap fortress as Andijan when the opportunity offered to win back the capital of his glorious ancestor, Timur.

As he drew near Samarkand, he learned that the

man who swings the sword of conspiracy must beware its double edge. The representatives of the Tarkhans, who were suspicious of Sultan Ali, came to meet him. They suggested coming to an understanding with a very influential *khoja*, Muhammad Yahia, who was their man in the city though the same who had formerly granted asylum to Ali. This *khoja*, they said, could put him in possession of Samarkand without the wasting of a single arrow. Baber, willing enough to have their support, consented.

On nearing the capital, this message came from Muhammad Yahia: "Come! Samarkand is yours!" Baber stealthily moved forward at nightfall to enter the city; but a deserter divulged the plan, and he was forced to retire.

On the heels of this, the unattached Khan of the Uzbek Turks—Shaibani Khan—captured Bokhara, a fief of his old protectors the Tarkhans. At this juncture, the mother of Sultan Ali, herself an Uzbek, enamoured of the Turk's handsome savagery, informed the Khan that if he would marry her she would deliver Samarkand to him as her dowry—on condition that he settled an appanage upon Ali. No need for a second invitation. Shaibani suddenly appeared beneath the walls of the town with his army and camped by the Garden of the Plains.

But Sultan Ali had no mind to fall in with the schemes of his mother. That night, without telling anyone of his plan, he paid his enemy an amicable visit to arrange matters more to his satisfaction. He was received without honour and put to death on the spot.

"And so," Baber wrote, "he ignominiously perished, through having been too much attached to a miserable few brief days of power."

As for his mother, "who in her frenzy to be married had thrown the interests of her son and her family to the winds," Shaibani treated her as a common concubine. And seized Samarkand—her dowry.

This Shaibani, or Shahi Beg, got scant praise from Baber, who described him as a nobody, from nowhere in particular. The grudge of the unlucky player !—one rarely shown by Baber. In reality, Shaibani was one of the remarkable men of his time, a descendant in the tenth generation from the eldest son of Genghis Khan. His grandfather had been an all-powerful noble, Lord of all Turks between the Lake of Balkash and the Urals, who had taken from one of his predecessors the name of "Uzbek." Toward the end of his life a large number of his subjects had left him to shift for themselves, forming the new federation of the Kazaks. This he faced in a great battle that brought him death (1469). Three years later the Mongol, Yunas Khan, crushed and dispersed the remainder of the Uzbeks, apparently wiping them off the map of Asia.

Shaibani, then twenty-one years of age, wandered for some time in the plains, vainly seeking friends, repose, shelter and food. Reduced at last to hopeless destitution, he and a handful of his partisans took refuge with the family of the Tarkhans, who gave him hospitality first at Bokhara, then in Turkestan. He followed Sultan Ahmed in a campaign undertaken by that king of Samarkand to wrest Tashkent from Mahmud Khan

By means of an adroit piece of treachery, Shaibani won the victory for the Khan, and received as a reward the city of Kurkestan which had been wrested from Ahmed in 1488. There on the extreme edge of his ancestral steppes, he commenced to rally about him the old following of his grandfather. They formed the core of what was soon to be a formidable body. Mahmud Khan, now weak in his powers of statecraft and warfare, thought he could use the young giant for his own ends. He would fling him at Samarkand, the perpetual goal of his sterile desires, flattering himself that Shaibani, the conqueror, would remain Shaibani, the grateful vassal.

But the fortunes of his protége had derived from his own misfortunes : in a short while, the latter would force him into Mongolia and put an end to his life. In the meantime, because of the enamoured widow, Shaibani could dispense with the Khan's patronage.

Once in Samarkand, Shaibani grew into a menacing thunder-cloud. His unexpected rivalry caught Baber in a very weak position. Tanbal, who had pretended to be reconciled with him, now remained behind at Farghana and sneeringly dispatched him a hundred useless men, unwilling to do more and too politic to do less. Others with him also recognized the thunder-cloud, and hastened to beg leaves of absence, which Baber granted, content to be rid of such questionable allies. So that at last he was left at most two thousand soldiers of his own principality, and a small troop of Tarkhans, who in losing Bokhara had lost much of their enthusiasm.

Knowing himself too weak to attack, the prince retreated in the direction of Hissar, which was at the time under the control of Khosrau Shah. And the instant they came within the realm of that wealthy ruler, part of his men deserted to the Shah, as irresistibly drawn to his service as fragments of steel to a magnet. As flies to carrion, was Baber's view ; for the creature was a stench in his nostrils.

He turned to thoughts of another uncle, Ahmed Khan, in Mongolia ; but to reach him he would have had to traverse Khosrau Shah's territory. He therefore renounced that plan and in desperation fell back until he had reached the mountains far to the north. Then he disappeared into the vast gorges, a last hazardous scheme in his head.

He lost heavily ; in the freezing winter beneath the peaks his horses and camels fell by the way. His men were half-frozen. But he went stubbornly on, aiming at the high pass of Sarytagh. When finally he reached it, the breath and sight of it completed what the hardships had begun ; the spirit of many of his men was broken, and they turned and rode away from their prince and the death he courted. So that when at last he won over the mountains and descended toward the valley of the Samarkand River, he had but two hundred left to command—a vagabond adventurer without lands or subjects, a chief of bandits rather than a sovereign lord.

But Shaibani knew that, destitute or not, Baber would return. After garrisoning Samarkand with six hundred men-at-arms, which he thought sufficient, he camped in the plains beyond the city with his nine thousand savage Uzbeks, and waited.

To advance upon him was to invite annihilation. But to retreat was to strip oneself naked before a like fate. The prince had nothing to lose. And he held to his desperate plan ; he would advance, and he would take Samarkand.

In the mountains after supper, as they warmed themselves against the cold, he would talk cheerfully with his men, jesting. "How long before we enter our good city, do you think?" he would ask the gallant two hundred. And they, not being men to kill their bear until they had sold the skin, would answer, three weeks, six months, a year. One of them, in his scorn for nine thousand Uzbeks, said, "A fortnight!" And his guess was recalled later, for it happened that he was right.

On that particular night Baber had a dream. He saw the Khoja Abaïd Allah, the old spiritual comforter of his father, who said to him, "Sheik Maslahat has given you..." and then vanished. Now Sheik Maslahat had been in his day a man noted for holiness. Nothing else was needed to confirm the hopes of the young soldier. He, of course, added to the verb "has given" its proper object, "Samarkand," which the *khoja* evidently had forgotten.

There came a time, finally, when his little force rolled their tents, looked to their bowstrings and their coats of mail. and then rode away from their hill camp at midday. Shaibani still awaited them at the valley-mouth with his army, a few miles to the north of the city—waiting for the mouse to come out of his hole.

He was confident, for there was only one exit, he thought. But Baber had trained as a cragsman, and his men were an iron remnant that had survived incredible hardship. Leaving the valley higher up, they scaled the almost impossible foothills, slipped past the Khan's flank five miles to the west, and before nightfall were under the walls of Samarkand while Shaibani sat watching his useless trap.

At midnight Baber ordered seventy of his trusted men to scale the ramparts near the Grotto of the Lovers. The garrison within slept. Once over the walls, the seventy moved silently to the Turquoise Gate, stabbed the guards there as they dozed, and toward three in the morning threw back the great iron-studded leaves of the portal to the rightful prince of Samarkand. Baber entered with a shout, and overwhelmed the napping garrison before they could offer a single blow.

A few merchants and craftsmen who had been awakened by the noise appeared at their doors. They wondered sleepily, then were astonished.

"It is the Sultan Baber!" they called to him as he rode past. "To you the salaam, lord! The Divine will has brought you here... May the Shadow of Your Presence be over our heads forever!"

With full morning the bazaar awoke and was overjoyed at the news. The crowd applauded their gentle prince, happy at seeing again that elegant person of the familiar miniatures, so handsome, so different from the uncouth, barbarous looking Uzbeks! Their pleasure was unbounded. As he rode through them beneath the cool arched ways of the market, they showered gifts upon him. "Here, lord, is a large turban of the finest muslin bordered with lace!" "Behold! Two matchless turquoise rings for the hand of my lord!"

It mattered little that in the general disturbance a few depraved rascals broke into houses whose owners were shouting happily in the streets. Let them rob! The prince had come back to them! Congratulations were the breath of the day as citizens hurried to the cheering spectacle of the favourite's return. All made haste to laugh before it became necessary to weep. They were in such good humour that they dug out all of the Uzbeks and mauled them with clubs and bashed them with stones until four hundred of them were dead. The rest they drove out of the town.

Toward sundown Shaibani, having been at last warned of the trick, came up with a hundred and fifty men to the Iron Gate just as Baber arrived to post his guard. It was the sole opportunity Baber ever had of doing away with his enemy; but with only twenty men it was one he could not grasp. Neither rival could strike; and Shaibani, recognizing this, turned and rode away unmolested.

Baber was now about to understand the intent of the saying, "They who win Samarkand must hold her against the desire of the world."

He looked about for resources to secure his prize, and found none. She had been ruined by continuous wars, she had practically no soldiers left, her tradesmen could not fight, her granaries were all but exhausted. From his Azure Palace Baber looked upon a city whose very beauty was a peril.

He was disquieted. He sent embassies to all of the neighbouring princes to ask for help, emphasizing the dangers to which their civilization was exposed by the invasion of the nomads.

But the debonair lad of eighteen did not inspire confidence in the hearts of fighters. Some, like the mighty Padishah of Herat, flatly refused to listen. Others, like the good uncle from Tashkent, no longer under illusions about Shaibani, sent reinforcements that were ridiculous in size ; no one put himself out seriously. The city did, however, receive reinforcements from the deserters of the tricked army, from repentant refugees, from adventurers and from new and conditional vassals. And the small villages and oases tendered their submission one after the other, until Shaibani had to retire to Bokhara.

Winter passed. Baber, with his customary audacity —the keystone of all his strategy—resolved to take the offensive. In the month of May, 1501, he marched down the river that flows from Samarkand to Bokhara and took up his position at Saripul, his right wing on the river. Shaibani appeared, and Baber engaged with him immediately, without waiting for the reinforcements that were on their way to join him.

The reason for his haste was a curious one : the stars of the constellation Scorpio by chance lay exactly between the two armies. Had he waited, they would have swung behind and over the enemy, opposing him full face—unfavourable sign! In his Memoirs he admits with a good grace that the consideration was rather worthless.

He attacked the centre of Shaibani's forces ; but Shaibani, following the age-old tactics of the Turks, bore down heavily upon his left wing, flung it back, crumpled it up, and won the day. Baber and fifteen of his men, mounted upon horses that were heavily armoured, plunged into the river and—despite their terrific weight—succeeded in crossing. They returned to Samarkand that evening alone.

Baber defended the place gallantly when his foe came up. But the investment was so close that the inhabitants had no chance to gether any of the new harvest and bring it in. Gaunt with hunger, they had to eat the meet of dogs and donkeys. The siege continued. No succour arrived ; the distress became intolerable, soldiers and civilians began to flee. And Baber capitulated in September, obtaining his freedom by a promise that his sister Khansadeh should marry Shaibani.

As for the populace, they were glad to be eating once more. They went about their daily tasks, they spun their fabrics, engraved their leathers, and hammered their bronzes, not unduly troubled that yesterday's master was not to-day's. Their lords varied like the seasons. The sufferings of the past already forgot, they merely glorified Allah for the fine picture that had lately graced the divine screen.

The golden domes and the palaces of blue porcelain were dull in the hue of midnight when Baber, with his mother and two of her ladies, rode secretly out the gates of Samarkand, toward the empty plains. The gigantic inscription that belted the dome of Timur's mausoleum was obscured by the night. Otherwise its strange letterings might have seemed to convey not the praise of God, but a reminder that Fortune was never more faithless than when she wore Samarkand as her jewel. Looking behind him, in regret as sharp as his fear, the prince rode without a halt until the next night, ate a meal of roasted horse-flesh and, after having allowed the mounts to breathe, spurred on again until he reached the oasis of Jizak.

Then there was abundance of rich food, white bread, apricots and grapes . . . and rest. ' In all my life," he says, "I have never enjoyed such contentment and tranquillity as I found there. I breathed freely once more, and the menacing image of death was dispelled from my eyes."

For he had believed himself pursued, in spite of the terms of his surrender. Why, he never tells us. If his enemies had been hunting him down, how could he have thought himself secure in a little oasis that was only seventy miles from Samarkand ? And if he had been given free conduct, why did he leave behind a part of his family ?

Jizak, the haven of rest, lay on the edge of the Mongol territories. Its proximity reminded Baber that he had uncles. He therefore left his mother and all of his goods at the village of Dahket, in the foothills of the mountains to the south and paid a visit to his relative at Tashkent, hoping that he would be given a province to govern. But Mahmud Khan feared Shaibani too heartily to aid his nephew ; and the vagrant prince had to return to Dahket undeceived.

Winter came. He spent his leisure in making long marches by himself, as though he were in himself an army, his feet bare, his body ill-protected by ragged clothing, hardening himself to the sharp stones and rough crags of mountains. Presently an incursion of Shaibani's forced him to take refuge among those same peaks. Upon a block of stone near a spring that was sacred to the natives of that high country, he cut these verses of Saadi's, which recalled to him the melancholy of his own fate :

Many have refreshed themselves like you,
Later to quaff a sweeter drink and die.
Pause ! Though by valour you subdue the world,
What in the world is yours when in your tomb ?

The descendant of the great emperors lived by brigandage, became nothing but a rover of the highways, without friends or home.

Realizing that such a life led nowhere, Baber returned in the spring to his uncle, with whom he dragged on a miserable and humiliating existence. The prince of Timur's line had apparently shot his bolt. He would never ride in triumph through Persepolis ! The men of Mahmud Khan's entourage scorned him. He was abandoned by his very servants; his entire cortége when he was received in audience consisted of two retainers.

To console himself, he turned to poetry, and wrote his first ghazal beginning :

I have found but one faithful friend—
But one confessor may I trust—my heart.

CHAPTER FOUR

A PRINCE OF THE MOUNTAINS

THE future was as dark as a wolf's mouth. In disgust, Baber was on the point of emigrating to the ends of China, when out of the black sky arrived his Mongolian uncle, Ahmed Khan, younger brother of Mahmud and master of an immense dominion that stretched for a thousand miles from the Lake of Balkash to Turfan and beyond.

Unlike his brother, he was made as the desert makes a man, crude as a nomad's tent, gross in manner, uncultivated in speech, and so formidable in swordplay as to have earned the title "Alatsha, Slayer of Kalmucks." But beyond that he was a rare philanthropist and gave a fifth of all his revenues to charity and to pious works. In the present instance, he showed his regard for his nephew by presenting him with one of his own horses fully caparisoned, a Mongol bonnet corded with gold, a Chinese robe of brocaded satin, a Chinese girdle from which hung rich seals, a purse, boxes of perfume and many precious amulets.

This unexpected arrival, a veritable windfall to Baber, was in effect to rescue Mahmud Khan from Shaibani. The latter, who was now the lord of Samarkand, Bokhara and Turkestan, and head of a strong army of fifty thousand men, had thought to follow up his success by crushing his former benefactor. Ahmed Khan had come to alter his opinion if he could.

The Khans, leaving at Tashkent and Uratepe two divisions to withstand the threatened attack of Shaibani, marched with about thirty thousand men to take Farghana from Tanbal, who was holding it in the name of Jahangir, Baber's young brother. Here, they felt, their eldest nephew might be of valuable assistance.

They put him in command of a small squadron with which he was to occupy the country south of the Syr river. Very soon the whole of the territory, Andijan alone excepted, submitted to its former prince. Emboldened by his success, he struck an audacious blow at the capital itself.

In the middle of the night he suddenly appeared at the oasis and dispatched some of his leaders to negotiate with the recalcitrant Tanbal. That worthy's surprise was complete and surrender was immediately agreed upon. Unfortunately, Baber could not accept it when it came. For, as he sat on his horse, awaiting the return of the messengers, the clash of war-cymbals rang out in the darkness.

Panic ! Flight ! Baber strove in vain to turn his cowardly followers back with his whip. The entire company fled away into the night ; and alone with two or three stout hearts, he remained to face the assumed enemy.

They were Mongol friends.

Five or six days later, Baber returned to take the place by storm. He repulsed a sortie of the garrison, drove them back within their gates with considerable loss, and might have carried on a successful assault that night, if only he had not been persuaded to wait until morning.

Dawn came, and with it an unexpected attack under Tanbal himself. Baber would have been taken had he not been in the habit of sleeping fully clothed. As it was, there was an excellent display of swordmanship between the prince, protected only by a helmet, and a host of horsemen armed at every point. An arrow pierced his thigh, a fierce blow from the sabre that he had recently presented to Tanbal split his casque. But he managed to disengage and flee to Osh.

The interrupted campaign was resumed. Again Andijan was besieged, this time by the Khans, who now dispatched their nephew to the other side of the river to seize Akhsai from Tanbal's brother. A complicated intrigue got Baber secretly into the town, where he effected a reconciliation with Jahangir. There followed the capture by treachery of Tanbal's brother; and lastly some brisk street-fighting at the foot of the citadel, during which Baber's small troop fared badly. When things were at their worst, Tanbal arrived with reinforcements and scattered the prince's men.

Riding furiously through the street, Baber was barely able to get clear of the gates with a handful of his men. They rode at full gallop down the rocky ravines, where a careless hoof meant a crushed skull, and by a steep trail climbed to the plateau that dominated the right bank of the Syr.

From the height of a small hill they saw a heavy

cloud of dust, raised by their pursuers. Thinking them more numerous than they really were, the fugitives turned and spurred on. Baber's horse foundered under him. One of his companions reined in and sprang off his mount, and Baber leaped into the saddle and went on. He killed three horses in succession, each time taking another from a loyal retainer. Finally there remained with him but one man, Mirza Kuli Kukuldash; and the top speed of their mounts had become a staggering walk.

"Living or dead," Baber said to his friend, "we shall not separate."

"My horse is done for," answered Kukuldash. "Don't trouble about me! Go as far as you can! Ride on!"

Baber pushed on alone. As the day ended, he had nearly reached a place of absolute safety and refuge, the high mountains, when his horse lurched beneath him and fell. Extricating himself, he rose wearily to his feet and looked back.

Two of his pursuers were at his heels, though separated from him by a deep ravine. They shouted to him, "Where are you going? There's no reason for flight. We have ridden to tell you that your two brothers have been taken prisoner!" The news puzzled him and he returned to answer. Then the two spoke to him deferentially, assuring him that Tanbal meant to proclaim him king. "The night is black, the desert is without roads, and we are at your service to lead you wherever you will." And they swore to the honour of their words.

"Very well," said Baber, "...but ride ahead of me."

They guided him down the ravines and torrents until, early in the morning, they came to a central highway, probably that which led to Tashkent over the Kindir Pass. One of them made a reconnaissance. He returned with the news of an oasis, but declared that it was impossible to ride to it over the road because there were too many troops abroad.

"But we cannot remain without food, nor can our horses. Hide under the cliff yonder, lord, while I go to the next village and get provisions for us."

He was gone for what seemed an unnecessarily long time. The sun was high when at last he returned... with nothing for the horses, and only three small loaves of bread for themselves. They must find pasturage for the animals. And a safer shelter for the prince! Suspicious-looking fellows had appeared from time to time on the road.

There was news, however, of a certain secluded garden on the edge of the oasis where no one would think of searching for the prince. Skirting the highway, following the mountain stream that divided Farghana from Tashkent, they reached it safely. The wind was cold; but Baber found shelter in a ruined hut. There he discovered an old sheepskin coat. Donning it, he built a fire and boiled himself a mess of millet—this future Emperor of India.

The next day, toward noon, one of his companions, who was standing his watch before the hut, announced the arrival of a public official called Yussuf. It was then that fear, his surest retainer now, knocked at Baber's heart. The officer did not conceal the fact that he had been sent by the brother of Tanbal.

"Speak out frankly," said Baber. "If I must prepare for the worst, at least give me time to offer up my last prayers."

Yussuf swore that there was nothing to fear. Nevertheless, the young prince withdrew to a secluded spot near a fountain where he performed the rites of ablution and made ready, with prayer, for the death which he thought inevitable, repeating with the poet:

What difference if we live a day or a hundred years?
Life is a palace lost when Death appears!

Then, with astonishing coolness he surrendered to sleep. But, while he slept, he beheld in a dream the grandson of the holy man, Obaïd Allah, who said to him, "Take heart! My grandsire has not forgotten you. He watches over you in every hour of need. Awake!" Baber opened his eyes on that note of warning and walked back to the hut in deep thought. When he came to the door of it, he overheard Yussuf and his companions plotting to seize and strangle him.

At that moment the sound of hoofs rang down the road. "Your enemies!" cried Yussuf.

The noise came nearer, then ceased. A jangling of spurs. Two men entered and threw themselves at the feet of the prince. They were two of his most devoted followers who had come to his rescue with twenty horsemen. The first one told how, when he had been separated from Baber in his headlong flight from Akhsai, he had gone to Andijan and had entered the city with the victorious Khans; and how in a dream Obaïd Allah had told him where he might find his prince and had commanded him to go to him.

"And now to horse! You must not be found here. Treachery is in the air."

And because winter was on them in full rigour, and because meat and forage could not be found elsewhere, Baber knew that he must return to Andijan. And so he mounted with them and rode away. Nor was it hard for the wanderer to remember that he had not eaten for two days. At noon, therefore, near Kernan, they caught a sheep, roasted and ate it, and rode with appetites appeased. In one day and two nights, halting just five times, they reached his capital. And there he remained with his uncles through the four months of snow.*

* See Appendix A.

CHAPTER FIVE

THE STIRRUPS OF RESOLUTION

SPRING came. The ice melted; and with it dissolved the military calm. In response to Tanbal's appeal, Shaibani mobilised an army of thirty thousand. enormous for that epoch and that country.

But when he looked about for a foe worthy of his mettle he was disappointed; for the Khans were in great distress. Their weakness was only too apparent. The cities revolted against their garrisons, whose brutality had exceeded all bounds. The country grew more and more hostile. With its leaders in something of a panic, therefore, the Mongol army retreated in haste toward Khojent, obviously meaning to use Tashkent as a base of operations. But the Khans, for some unknown reason, changed their plans and marched to the east, toward Namangan. A single suggestion dropped by Baber leads us to suppose that they intended fighting a safe rear-guard action on their way back to Mongolia.

But whatever uncertainty might have veiled their plans, there was little doubt of Baber's position. He knew that he had nothing more to expect at their hands. Still he would not desert them, for he was a man of his word. He could not in conscience separate from them without a clear cause. They had not yet been decisively beaten, and the Uzbek general had not made any positive threat since the autumn campaign.

Both of these possibilities were now about to be realized simultaneously.

The occasion was ripe. The Khans, as may be remembered, had left two divisions of their troops at Tashkent and Uratepe, thinking them sufficient to check the Uzbek offensive should it attempt to block the Mongol retreat. As a consequence, their forces were scattered, the main body numbering not over fifteen thousand.

Shaibani struck with the speed of lightning and the cunning of a hawk. It was a charge rather than a march. Under cover of darkness he slipped between the two Mongol divisions, feigned an attack upon Uratepe to hold one of them there, and then bolted away the same night.

At Arkhian, three miles west of Namangan, he overtook the Khans at the same moment as the couriers sent to warn them, fell upon their troops in the grey of dawn before they had time even to form line of battle, and routed them, June, 1503. Then, taking the two Khans prisoners, he proceeded by forced marches to Tashkent, captured it, laid the entire province at his feet, and enrolled some thirty thousand Mongols in his army. The rest gained their eastern steppes, and the banks of the Syr were freed for ever from Mongol domination.

The Uzbek lord was magnanimous towards his two captives. "I owe my conquests to you; in return I give you your life and liberty." To discount the cost of his generosity, however, he stipulated that his house be united in marriage with the Jagatai. He selected the daughter of Mahmud Khan as his son's wife, and for himself chose the youngest sister of Baber's mother. Baber's own eldest sister, it will be recalled, had been the price of the prince's freedom at Samarkand. But might is of no value unless it is based upon right; and the greater the right the greater the might. Shaibani was adding to his grains of legitimacy.

The younger of the two Khans, Ahmed, won back to his far-away pastures in Mongolia, where he died of chagrin a few months later. The Sheik-ul-Islam said to him one day:

"If it is true that Shaibani Khan has poisoned Your Highness, then permit me to find a powerful antidote which will cure Your Highness."

"Yes," Ahmed replied, "Shaibani has poisoned me. And I shall tell you how. That man, who rose from the lowest dunghill to the highest rank, took me prisoner and then dared to set me free! My blood has turned to the upas-milk of shame. If you know of an antidote against that poison, give it to me!"

Mahmud, the elder, survived his brother a number of years, likely enough because of his habitual indolence. He was distrusted by his Mongols; harassed by truceless quarrels with his nephews. The waste tract in the Jagatai country given him to rule wearied him. He would rather have been a washer of pots at Tashkent than a king in the desert. So, he returned one day to Farghana to place himself under the protection of Shaibani.

"To grant mercy once is wise; but to grant it twice

is foolhardy!" said the latter, and ordered Mahmud's throat to be cut (1508).

Baber had participated in the fatal battle at Namangan (Arkhian). Good luck was with him once again in the saddle, and he managed to escape. But when he sought to ride into the north, he found the road guarded by Shaibani's patrol, posted there to catch him. He turned to the south and, following hidden ways, succeeded in reaching the mountains that rose above Khokan on this side of Farghana. There he found a precarious refuge for himself and a small band, comprising his mother, his family, a few men-at-arms, and his servants.

For a year he lived the life of a Highland rebel out of Walter Scott. Beneath peaks of ice nineteen thousand feet high stretched a dismal solitude of shattered rock and thin pasturage, pitted with headlong torrents and dark valleys, where the Kirghiz shepherd-brigands pitched their tents of black felt and watched their flocks of sheep and yaks, their herds of camels and horses. Here and there at great intervals a village huddled in the shelter of the cliff—a dozen makeshift huts of grey clay. They were gloomy dwellings that smelled of must, sour milk and ageless filth. Poorly constructed, their foundations would rot from under them, if the spring rains failed to wash them apart.

All this made it a sad year of privation and distress for Baber. Yet, for all that, the country had its virtues: it was an almost secure haven for a fugitive. His enemies hesitated to pursue him over those precipitous rock-rimmed trails that led to no booty worth the name—only livestock that grazed high up on the mountains, with the Kirghiz keeping sharp watch. They were proud to protect the noble representative of their race, the sacred blood of their legendary ancestor; and, when danger threatened him, to hide him among their impenetrable crags.

Besides, Shaibani was very busy beyond the mountains, in Hissar. At the moment Fortune hung fire. Shaibani had no time to waste upon an outcast royal stripling.

Sheep-herding gave his young rival plenty of occasion for thought. Though scarcely out of adolescence, Baber had already sampled the dregs from the cup of human fate. Yesterday a prince upon the throne of the great Timur, to-day he was a pitiful vagabond, an encumbrance upon the earth. He had learned in a hard school that faith could be inconstant, and friends treacherous, that cowardice would serve for the breaking of an oath and that loyalty was a slight thing compared with self-interest. And now he could write:

What faith can one put in the things of this world, my heart?

What good can you hope for from souls that ignore the truth?

All his pain, all his labour, all his planning throughout seven years, had sufficed only to put upon the throne of his father that blockhead Tanbal, and upon the lordly throne of his Samarkand a Shaibani, a barbarian, a desert robber whose fortunes had been born from the pity of his friends and who had waxed fat upon treachery and ferocity.

Truly, the poets had been right to phrase in a thousand forms the illusion that is life. What use the room of a Darius or a Xerxes in this ruinous caravanserai of a night ? If a vestige of glory linger, it could scarce be more than a name traced upon a wall, a mere name that one scratch of a fingernail could erase.

It would be wrong, however, to suppose that such thoughts sickened Baber of action. On the contrary, they showed him how unimportant are danger and the risk of life. He was an athlete contesting in a field of sports : he had tried to play skilfully, to bear away the glorious prizes, Samarkand and Herat. Now, the game ended, carelessly he flung into the face of the world the vanity of all glory—a handful of ashes.

The philosopher was not dozing, in spite of his verses upon futility. Through the long months he watched vainly for an occasion to begin his career afresh. Singly his friends would ride down from the mountains, travelling by night and hiding by day, mingling with trade-caravans, deserters and beggars, gathering news. But for a long time they returned with downcast faces. Nothing seemed to shake the power of the present masters.

At last came heartening words : Shaibani had decided to sweep out Tanbal, an uncertain vassal, and was preparing a great expedition against him. Baber judged it inexpedient to wait for a better opportunity of escape. He reflected that nothing more was to be gained from gnawing his crust like a beggar in this unknown hole and that it was infinitely better to be in the saddle, no matter where, than to die obscure in bad odour, among savages.

His chance had come. In marching upon Farghana, Shaibani had left Hissar open to him. Baber resolved to go in that direction in an attempt to reach the court of his great cousin, Sultan Hussayn Mirza, at Herat. This sovereign was the generally acknowledged head of the Timurids, successors of Timur, and the only one to bear the title of Padishah.* Baber's plan, really, was a pretext for action. How else overtake that destiny which waits for the man who seeks it ?

In his own picturesque phrase, he "at once set his feet in the stirrups of resolution." It was June of 1504 and he was barely twenty. With a band of two or three hundred men, women and children, he proposed to cross mountains higher than the Alps, a barrier that rose sheer, forbidding, between the basins of the Syr and of the Amu (Oxus). It was an undertaking that would have daunted Hannibal. Ill-defined trails led to the passes. There was nothing but narrrow galleries crowded by glaciers and beetling peaks ; twelve thousand feet up in cloudland, they were all but impassable with snow and ice. But with Baber leading, while his men broke the way for the women and children, the little band toiled bravely to the top of the world, then down, down into the valley of the Surkhab, a monstrous gash fifteen thousand feet deep.

They were now in the land of Karateghin, through which in the time of the Roman Empire passed the silk caravans on their year-long journeys from China

* Corresponding roughly to the title of Emperor in the European Middle Ages.

to Babylon and Tyre. When Baber halted for the second stage of his journey, near Hissar, he had covered two hundred and twenty miles through territory as difficult as any on earth because of the pitch of its roads and the poverty of its resources.

His company was more wretched than the most ragged pack of gypsies. Though few, they were still too numerous to live off the country, and their equipment was ridiculously inadequate. They were clothed as their race is to-day : the body wrapped in a cotton mantle with long sleeves, open at the front and held by a twisted belt at the waist ; on their feet, boots of rawhide which tore into shreds after a few days' wear on sharp stones. For the whole three hundred they had but two tents, both of them reserved for the women. Baber himself slept in his quilted jacket beneath a lean-to made of laths covered with bark, which was set up at every encampment. But he let nothing interfere with the ceremonial first shave prescribed, according to the Turkish custom, for his birthday, the twenty-third by the lunar calendar. Nor did it prevent him from moving indomitably on, this man of twenty years, four months and six days—calendar of Gregory.

At that time Khosrau Shah, under the suzerainty of Hussayn Baikara, ruled at Hissar and Kunduz over the entire valley of the Amu, between the mountains of Farghana and the Hindu Kush. From north to south and again from east to west, his appanage measured two hundred and fifty miles. He was a Turk of the Kipchaks, of the lesser nobility, and regarded by Baber as an intruder.

He had been at first a favourite of the Tarkhans, the *grands seigneurs* of Samarkand ; then he had gone over to Mahmud Mirza, uncle to Baber. A *mignon* of his successive masters, he was promoted rapidly. Under Sultan Mahmud he had become a most puissant lord, and his depravity had enlarged that monarch's conception of debauchery. It was a common story that when the latter was in residence at Samarkand the tradesmen never dared go out and leave their young sons alone in the house.

The curses of afflicted hearts rose against him. And Baber, recalling the verse of Saadi, "One sigh of the oppressed can shake the world," notes that this evil prince lasted only six months as lord of Samarkand.

Until that fatal moment, however, Khosrau Shah employed his time profitably. As governor of Kunduz, he gathered around him a vast retinue and amassed a huge treasure, employing both to further his ambitious schemes.

The son of Mahmud, Baisonkor, after losing Samarkand, had received from him a lavish welcome that seduced the ingenuous lad, whose good-nature was too often fuddled with wine. He had been treacherously induced by his host to march against his eldest brother, Masoud, in order to supplant him in the principality of Hissar. In a swirling dusty battle the two brothers met. Masoud was defeated and taken as a captive to Kunduz. There Khosrau had him blinded. Then he strangled Baisonkor with his own hands by means of the usual bowstring. Thus rid of the troublesome sons of his benefactor, he usurped their heritage, which he had now held for five years.

Baber's hatred of the parvenu, the murderer of his two cousins, was only too well justified. Indignantly he expressed his opinion of such hideous deeds, done at the behest of a miserable ambition for the "possession of this life of but five days," from which poor sum one must even subtract the days of one's birth and one's death.

So low an opinion of worldly distinction is surprising perhaps in a man who spared no effort to advance himself, who burned out his life in conquering new realms and shaping a great empire, who had himself used violence to dispossess Baisonkor, his cousin-german. Nevertheless, there was here no conscious hypocrisy. He no more scrupled to exert his power in the defeat of a rival than champion oarsmen do when employing all their muscle and skill to win from weaker opponents. But, with him, force did not exclude benevolence, or some measure of loyalty, or gentleness. Treachery, underhand trickery and needless cruelty were repugnant to him. Assassination was never his way of achieving a given end. It was not playing the game. No reward seemed great enough to offset infamy.

The forlorn wanderers had been able to endure their foretaste of hell in the hope of obtaining comparative easement at the hands of Khosrau Shah. They were to find him as inhospitable as the mountains behind them. Worse, he laughed at their rags and was infinitely bored by the account of their hardships.

It suited him to send as ambassador to their chief a man of no rank whatever, whose duty was not to do them honour but keep guard on them and see them out of the country as quickly as possible. Baber felt outraged. He should have looked for no better treatment from an enemy; but in his pride of birth he had expected a certain amount of consideration as his royal due. Besides, Khosrau Shah was reputed vain of his reputation for liberality.

Undeterred by the chill reception, Baber went on his way, better in health and more cheerful because of the rumours of his popularity among the people. For the local underlords and soldiers despised the upstart grandiosity of their own master. They took a lively interest in the transit of this adventurous prince. Was he not of glorious ancestry, a leader whose courage and ability had been proven many times?

Men who thirsted for action became restive when they heard of his coming; old forgotten fidelities were revived. Very soon some of his former lords re-entered his service. Khosrau's own brother presented himself along with his entire family. Baber's progress through Hissar became something of a triumph. His following increased daily. Finally the Mongols in the pay of Khosrau let the prince know that they were ready to fight under his standard; and little by little they came, swelling his forces.

With the River Amu at last behind him, Baber traversed the foothills of the Hindu Kush and descended into the deep valley of Khamerd, where he left in the stronghold of Hajir the women and children and those men that had broken under the strain of the recent ordeal. He was once more ready to attempt a tilt with fortune.

Whereupon his evil genius seemed about to visit him again. He was informed of the terrifying activity of Shaibani. The Uzbek chief had taken Andijan, had killed Tanbal and subdued Farghana, all in forty days. Now he was rushing headlong upon Hissar. An expedition led by him the previous year for the purpose of feeling the ground had shown him that Khosrau could be chased off with a single gesture, as a fly is frightened away from a plate. This time he was prepared for a decisive campaign. He occupied Hissar and sent an army corps against Kunduz, whence Khosrau had fled with all haste.

To appreciate the speed of Shaibani's movements, it is necessary to remember that Samarkand is two hundred and fifty miles from Hissar, and the latter one hundred and sixty miles from Kunduz.

Swift action is always impressive. Shaibani's was completely demoralizing, especially to the nominal sovereign of the province, in whose name the public prayers were read—Hussayn Baikara, the Timurid Padishah of Herat. Age had made him irresolute. Instead of directing against the invaders the vigorous offensive that Baber would have desired, the Padishah contented himself with reinforcing the garrisons along the road by which Shaibani might march against his capital.

That spelled the finish of his servant, Khosrau. His army scattered at the Uzbek approach like a heap of feathers before a violent wind. Baber, too, should have suffered from the debacle. Yet he did not. He profited by the extinction of one of his enemies; and he gained an army with which to protect himself from his still more dangerous foe. Quickly he collected the fragments of Khosrau's dispersed forces. Deserters poured into his camp. All the rest of the Mongols —four thousand men with their families—came to tender him their allegiance.

There was nothing left for Khosrau to do but surrender, either to Shaibani or to Baber. He chose the latter, and secured the guarantee of life and property.

Baber, still a somewhat bedraggled prince, seated upon the carpet of sovereignty beneath a broad plane tree at the foot of the gigantic mountains, received Khosrau's humble submission. He saw his enemy, omnipotent yesterday and an insolent usurper of royalty, dismount before him at the formal distance fixed by the great Timur, prostrate himself three times, approach to offer presents and to enquire thrice after the prince's health, then retire, facing the throne, and kneel thrice again. His nobles, his partisans and retainers, great and small, had deserted him; he who had once commanded thirty thousand warriors stood alone now, a little man, decrepit, humiliated, even his speech broken by the shock of fortune. Baber, lately Lord of Nowhere, now the head of an army, recited the twenty-fifth verse of the third *sura* of the Koran:

Oh, Allah! Kingship is thine alone;
Thine to give when thou pleasest;
Thine to take away at thy pleasure!

Then a brother of the two princes whom Khosrau Shah had assassinated claimed the traditional right of the avenger. But Baber, faithful to the word he had given, bade him respect the life of his enemy. Khosrau Shah was allowed to depart for Khorassan with his wealth—gold, silver, gems—heaped upon four trains of mules and camels.

At the same time the prince gave another proof of his natural generosity. His entourage advised him to get rid of his own brother, Jahangir, by sending him to Herat; for if he were allowed to remain, they insisted, he would become a focus of intrigues.

The counsel was wise. "Ten dervishes," said the proverb, "can sleep within the folds of the same robe, but two kings cannot live in the same kingdom." Baber refused to eject a man, who, though a traitor once, had been his loyal companion in his latest trials...He would live to regret his decision.

The means of independence now his, he no longer thought of taking refuge in Herat, the city of Asia's refugees. On the other hand, the too evident contrast between his small army and the redoubtable force of Shaibani did not encourage him to meet that vigorous man in battle just yet. He thought it wise to put a natural barrier between the two of them.

So he turned toward the city of Kabul, from which one of his cousins, Abd-ur-Razzak, had just been driven by a great noble of Afghanistan, Mukim. Who speaks of one man's trouble speaks of another's hope!

The distance was not very great, only a hundred miles or so. But the Hindu Kush, one of earth's most formidable mountain chains, stood between him and his objective. Less majestic, perhaps, than the Roof of the World, over to the east, still its peaks rose well over twenty thousand feet while its passes were twelve thousand in elevation.

Baber scaled them.

At the summit he halted and gazed into space. Low on the horizon of the evening sky, far away to the south, gleamed a star that was new to him. With an interest in astronomy appropriate in the nephew of the savant, Ulugh Beg, he inquired if it were not Suheil.*

"Aye," came the answer. "And remember, Sire, the words of the poet: 'Suheil! Fortunate is he on whom shines the light of your countenance!'"

* Our Canopus, brightest star in the southern hemisphere; the name used by Afghans to designate the south.

CHAPTER SIX

KABUL AND THE GATEWAY TO INDIA

DOWN the bleak gorges that trench the highlands between the Hindu Kush and Kabul poured the army of the indomitable Baber. It brushed aside with little effort the forces sent to guard the valley-mouths, and added to its strength every day from the Mongols and Turks who had fought under Khosrau. Presently Baber was at the head of an imposing array, estimated by Muhammad Haidar at twenty thousand.

The count is exaggerated perhaps; for in those times and countries, only rarely was an exact tally kept. Whatever the number, the prince had enough on his hands in checking the lust for marauding that flared up among his soldiers. Even at the outset of his career he had insisted upon discipline. Now, when he learned that one of his men had stolen a jar of oil from a native, he struck the offender down with his own hand before the royal tent. The example bore excellent fruit.

With Kabul in sight, a council was held to decide what course to pursue: whether they should undertake the siege of a place whose position rendered it capable of long resistance or whether, in the view of the lateness of the season, they should go into winter quarters.

Baber always consulted with his staff before undertaking any important step. It was not modesty, nor simply the desire to find out their opinions. It was a basic necessity; he had to know definitely that his men would follow him. On this occasion the council resolved upon action. Baber waited until his family, which had been in the stronghold of Hajir, rejoined him; then moved on and encamped within full view of the town.

Words proved easier than action. By no ordinary force of arms could he hope to capture the place. Once within the outlying orchards and vineyards, his army would have to ascend a long steep hill before it could reach the city proper. This slope was barren of all vegetation, and Baber knew that when rain fell it became a slide of liquid mud. If his soldiers did gain the top, they would find themselves balked by a moat twenty-five feet broad and sixteen feet deep, an expanse of green slime. Worse, beyond rose an immense earthwork two hundred and fifty feet from edge to unsheltered edge. No engineer could hope to tunnel through it to the walls. Finally, these walls commanded every angle of approach. Kabul seemed unassailable.

Baber, however, was wise beyond his years. It flashed upon him that it might be undermined from within. He planned, in other words, to breach the walls by intrigue rather than by catapult. He had reliable agents in the city, and negotiations were under way immediately. Grumblings soon arose in the garrison; half of the soldiers deserted. Stores of food were mysteriously put to the torch. Discontent spread among the people.

Whereupon the better to extinguish any hope of resistance that the townsmen might nurse, the former Lord of Samarkand staged an effective military demonstration. Over a hill directly opposite the citadel he marched his host of invaders, ensigns astream in the wind, horns braying, cymbals clashing, drums roaring.

Behind its parapets the town admired and quaked. The people now felt themselves at the mercy of foes both within and without. The usurper, Mukim, knowing their spirits unstrung, was obliged to surrender. As a reward for submitting to the inevitable, he was permitted to depart unmolested. Baber could afford to be generous, for at the cost of only six lives—men, whom he had executed in order to check pillaging—he had with extraordinary speed become potential master of all the lands between the Hindu Kush and Ghazni, a sweep of some hundred and fifty miles.

Less than four months before, he had been a ragged exile from his chilly, impoverished inheritance, Farghana. In that brief time he had transplanted his hearth and fortunes six hundred and twenty arduous miles to a domain which, if not wealthy, reached out towards the Indian Ocean.

Now came the ticklish matter of naming Kabul's proper lord. At the death of Abu Saïd, Baber's grandfather, in 1469, it had been given entirely into the keeping of his son, Ulugh Beg, who in turn had left it to his own legitimate successor in 1501. The latter, as noted above, had more or less invited Baber's intervention when ousted by a revolt of his nobles under Mukim, the Arghun. This Mukim was a Turco-Mongolian of non-royal blood who, by way of dignifying his usurpation, claimed descent from Genghis Khan.

Baber, by his capture of Kabul, had satisfactorily demonstrated that Mukim's pretensions were hollow. And now he restored the legitimate line by placing himself in the seat of government. The hawk of fortune was again upon his wrist.

His cousin, Abd-ur-Razaak, the rightful king, was no better off than before. But since in Afghanistan, then as now, a man's right to the throne was no stronger than the army at his back, no army meant no redress. This time the loser bowed to his fate, and was given a small estate for his good sense.

As for Baber, as soon as he had installed himself in his new kingdom, he divided the territory into fiefs which he distributed among the chieftains who had followed him. And those who had joined him last fared as well as the oldest in his service. The only ones to receive special consideration were the faithful few who had come with him from Samarkand, Hissar and Farghana in his flight from the Uzbeks. They were without anything, and to them he gave clothing and cattle as well as lands. And he added gold.

The expense of such open-handed generosity exceeded the earning power of a land which was more competent at warfare than at trade, and which merely laughed at the lists of the tax-collectors when they came peaceably. To gather up revenues in that country required the sword. Baber used it : a few sudden raids directed against recalcitrant lords and villages, and they hastened to do what they could for their king.

The returns still remained insufficient. Even when the prince himself sprang into the saddle and galloped off to collect in person, they did not satisfy his needs. The value of Kabul was not in its money-bags.

Yet never would he let slip from his hands this principality that he had wandered so far from his home to conquer. It was a poor city in a poor country, with its annual revenue equivalent to little more than thirty thousand pounds. Still, he would cling to it until the end, for it was without equal as a military post. It was to be the base of his future conquests, remain his favourite home and the setting of his happiest years, for which he would yearn among the luxuries of his southern empire. It was the spot where he would finally rest—under his tomb.

Kabul rises out of the plateau of Iran near its eastern extremity, where it descends in the manner of a gigantic stairway down to the torrid plains of India. Its natural defences are formidable, its position making it an almost impregnable fortress. To the east the land falls away steeply in a series of terraces that command the narrow gorges by which they are separated. It backs upon a huge rampart of mountains whose few passes are almost inaccessible and are snowbound for four or five months of the year.

Standing more than a mile above sea level, Kabul has a climate wholly different from that of other cities in the same latitude, say, Gibraltar or Los Angeles. Cold in winter, hot in summer, its temperature ranges from zero to one hundred and twelve degrees. The air is dry, luminous, pure ; and the fall of rain and of snow is confined to twenty-three days a year, abundant in March and light in April. The climate must have reminded Baber of Samarkand, save that in its most delightful season, autumn, Kabul was warmer.

The environs of the town smiled in green orchards within a frame of dark mountains from which to the north-west the snow never melted. To the south-west, the castle of the ancient kings crowned a hill mantled with gardens watered by a spring near which the immortal prophet Elijah had left his footprint. From its summit Baber loved to let his eyes dwell on the fresh meadows beyond the edge of the cultivated lands, beholding in fancy the northern plains from which his own race had sprung. Farther off, by the mouths of the clear torrents that gushed from the foothills of the Hindu Kush, stretched a chain of field-encircled villages like links of green-enamelled gold.

This valley, a brief rest in the overpowering symphony of the mountains, and so fragile in its grace, was nevertheless of major importance to Baber's world. It was the bridge between India and Persia. Caravans poured in from Herat and Ispahan, from Tabriz and Baghdad and the famous port of Ormuz, from Delhi, and Golconda, from Bengal and Vijayanagara, and from Samarkand, Bokhara, Farghana, Kashgar and even China. Every year the horses of the traders ran to no less than ten thousand. Baber called it the veritable warehouse of Hindustan, whence annually came nearly twenty thousand people with slaves, Indian fabrics, sugar, spices, every kind of merchandise, upon which the least greedy merchant might take a profit of four hundred per cent.

Baber's delight in the province was measureless. Travelling down the river from Kabul, following its channel, now broad, now narrow as it flowed between the Safed Koh and the tremendous bulwarks of the Hindu Kush, he came shortly to Nengnahar, whose deep valleys were never touched by snow. There he found another world where the trees, the flowers, the animals, and even the customs were peculiar to themselves. Rice, oranges and lemons flourished there. Later the banana and sugar cane were introduced from India by Baber. Upon the left bank of the river stood Lamghan, proud in the possession of the tomb of Lamech, the father of Noah, proud also of bearing his very name. Finer than anything in the neighbouring provinces of Kunar, Bajaur and Swat were their groves of oranges, lemons, pomegranates, coriander and date. Forests of cypress, oak, olive, and mastic, swarmed with countless numbers of birds and wild game, including peacocks and parrots, nilgais and monkeys.

The region boasted one particularly strange custom noted by Baber. At the death of a woman, her body was lifted to an open framework by four men of the religious community. If she had lived a pure and innocent life, her body would of its own accord throw itself to the earth ; otherwise it remained motionless. Fortunately for women, to whose failings history seldom closes her eyes, the Brethren of Mercy are usually far-seeing and understanding the world over. And in that country, apparently, they added *savoir-*

faire to *savoir-vivre.* Baber relates now a sultan of Bajaur who had lost his wife refused to weep for her until her virtue had been established in the customary fashion. Subjected to the test, the lady's body gave the required leap; whereupon the Sultan assumed the required mourning.

To the north the young conqueror mounted from the river valley into a thick, mountainous forest where pine and juniper replaced the oak, and the natives retained their pagan customs in spite of Islam. Farther on he found nothing but Kafirs, infidels with souls black like their garments, and so given to the sharp wine of their district that each man carried a leather bottle of it about his neck and drank of it on the march in place of water.

West of Kabul the oak-trees disappeared; even the pines were rare upon the barren highlands, and pasturage for the horses was to be found only along the beds of the small streams. Over to the south-west a great fan of mountains poured its waters into the dread marshes of Seistan—swamps formed by the melted snows, a green quagmire where there were no trails. Within it lay the basin of the Helmand River, an utterly flat country, monotonous to sadness and without vegetation, hiding only a single animal—the dun-coloured wild horse—and furnishing only a single shrub for firewood—the saksaul, which, being leafless, offered no shade.

At the bolt of the fan, seven thousand feet above the floor of the southern plains, the city of Ghazni raised its few houses of dried mud. A city? It was a sombre village in a sombre place, a hell upon earth that, one would think, might have induced the Creator to dispense with the other abode of torment. Baber was astonished that the famous Sultan Mahmud had chosen it, or at least retained it, as his capital.

For Mahmud had been a person of some importance. Five hundred years before, he had been the master of Afghanistan and Persia; he had overrun northern India and had conquered that part of it which lay to the west of Kashmir, Oudh and the Vindhya Mountains. He had been a truly great king, and at his court had resided the ornament of the world, the great Firdausi, the Homer of the Persians.

But Mahmud had been nearer to the nomadic traditions than was Baber. His lofty condescension to the artistic and literary amusements of his subjects had not altered the old campaigner's heart that beat within him. Wide, empty horizons alone touched that stern heart; he was happy in an unassailable retreat among the peaks.

Baber's new domain went but a little way further. It included only the most northerly, the most savage part of Afghanistan. And in that slight holding he ruled over a dozen races that spoke a dozen languages, formed of Persian, Turkish, Mongolian, Hindustani, the native Afghan dialect, and variants of all of them.

Law was as inchoate as language; brigandage was so universal that it broke orderly policies into fragments. At the foot of the Safed Koh existed such a ferocious alliance of outlaws that Baber was powerless to cope with them. Even at the end of his life, in the flower of his strength, he was still promising himself that something *would* be done about it.

The kingdom was obviously worth little in itself; but in its function it was of inestimable value. It was the gateway of India, the hawk's nest over against the hen-roost. Every conqueror who had ever invaded India passed that way into his conquests upon the peninsula: Alexander of Macedon, Antiochus the Seleucid, Menander the Graeco-Bactrian, the Yue-chi nomads from China, the Ephtalite Huns, Mahmud of Ghazni, Muhammad of Ghor and Timur of Samarkand.

Nowadays, in the light of far retrospect, we are tempted to think that once he had posted himself at Kabul, Baber was turned inevitably by the supreme quality of his genius toward the fabulous wealth of those valleys of the Indus and the Ganges. His fervid chroniclers wrote that everything drove him on, tradition and the lie of the land. He possessed, they said, the gate; he possessed the road, he possessed the claims of a descendant of Timur and the example of the Turkish race that with little intermission had been masters of India for more than a thousand years.

But in reality he hesitated a long time before taking such an irrevocable step. It was for him nothing more than a *pis-aller*. One might almost say that he became Emperor of India in spite of himself.

His ambition had always been to shine in a more familiar setting, to command the princes of his own house and to rule in the capitals of his own dynasty, Samarkand and Herat. Always his heart was stirred at the familiar customs and sights of his own land. His spirit found rest within the enchanted circle of the people and things of his boyhood, his native poets and his artists. The men of taste and learning who gathered about him always spoke his own tongue. His health and vigour bespoke his native climate, its rude winters and brief summers, the sharp freshness of its springs and the serene clarity of its autumns; the prairies and mountain torrents, the shade and the fruits of the gardens of home. Hindustan held in converse the emperor but never the man; it was to him only a land of exile.

Once in Kabul, however, necessity drove him into Hindustan on his first expedition. He went not because he foreknew his coming glory but because he wished to reconnoitre, and that his hungry state might fatten on the natural resources of the amazing plains to the south. He badly needed grain, cattle, stuffs for clothing, and all the many trinkets with which a general rewarded his men if he meant to keep their services. He might easily have marched in another direction, and would have done so had not his council thought that Hindustan would bring him the greatest profit.

He departed, then, in January, 1505, on his foray, by the usual route through Peshawar.

With the first ranges of mountains behind him he entered a world whose novelty amazed him, so different was it from his windy, high Farghana. Suddenly, in place of the temperate Asia he knew, and the half-European uplands of Anatolia and Iran, he found himself in an Asia of monsoons, of incredible heat and moisture, fit to snap the cords of bows and thews of men.

The Khyber Pass, thirty miles long, led him down into the valley of the Indus; and the raging sun blistered his men beneath their heavy jackets and coats of mail, and scorched the brain-pans of many a one. Exasperated by the vehemence of the heat, Baber was for crossing the river at once; but Baki Jaganiani, the most influential of his generals, warned him that the country was too difficult, too pestilential; and he turned south along the mountains to the east of the stream.

His soldiers pillaged everything in their path; they sacked and burned the houses, trampled the wheat and rice fields, and carried off the herds. Of cattle they took such a vast number that the share of the ordinary man in the ranks was three hundred head; the booty became unwieldy and was left behind almost as soon as it was gained—a terrific but unavoidable waste.

Once they had the good fortune to overhaul a large caravan. When the chief merchant had been beheaded the store was divided, and Baber's army marched thenceforward in a blaze of brocaded silks exotically perfumed with spice.

Such a blinding light could not be hid long under a bushel. The news spread widely over the plains that Timur had come again with death riding in his van. The Afghans flocked in with grass in their mouths in token of their submission. Such as attempted to defend their fortified rocks were treated to a murderous assault; and when the stubborn tribesmen had been captured, their heads were piled into conspicuous pyramids, to serve as monuments of wisdom for those that might wish to keep theirs on their shoulders.

A tiger hunting through light brush was not more

wary than the prince in that hostile country. His march had something of a crouch about it, he was ready for defence as well as attack. Every night a strict watch was kept, every corps was armed and in its place, and sentinels were posted about the entire camp an arrow's flight apart. Further to assure his army against surprise, Baber himself frequently went the sentry rounds at night.

Arrived at last on the plateau where the city of Dera Ghazi Khan now stands, the expedition swung to the west. Then the rains began. The men slept in water; there was no ground visible, and they rode their horses through one vast lake. Grain and forage disappeared from the face of the land, the starved horses dropped.

Yet all the fatigues and grumblings of his troops never moved Baber from his insatiable curiosity. The unfeigned and delighted wonder in his heart was fixed there, to vanish only with life itself. He saw everything. When he approached the shores of the lake of Ab-Istadeh it was twilight. He observed that the sky flamed and darkened by turns as if from an intermittent afterglow. The phenomenon was explained when, upon reaching the same lake, he noted immense flocks of wild geese, the underside of whose wings was a flaming red.

Near Ghazni someone pointed out to him the miraculous tomb of a saint, which had the habit of moving whenever prayers were recited before it. He visited the tomb and laid bare a pious fraud on the part of its guardians: a false and movable vault had been built over the sepulchre; when the monks slid it from one side to another, the very tomb appeared to stir. Baber had the old vaulting destroyed and replaced by a less spectacular but more honest one.

At last, after an absence of four months, he was back in Kabul, not yet a conqueror, but a very deeply impressed raider over five hundred miles of a rich land.

Financially the expedition had not been profitable. His men had plundered hugely, but they had wasted as hugely. They returned ill provided with booty, bare in equipment and temper. Many deserted and joined themselves with Baber's young brother, Nasir Mirza, who was preparing an army for Badakshan, to the north of the Hindu Kush, in answer to the invitation of the nobles in revolt there against Shaibani. The purge of their going was good for the health of Baber's troops; he could now feed and equip the men who remained.

He did well, for he was acquiring a reputation far away in India. Timur had returned! And he would need an excellent army to sustain that great mantle in a future as yet undreamed of.

During the months that followed, Baber conducted many similar forays, all of them shorter than the first, some of them undertaken in the dead of winter, when the horse that lost the trail sank in snow over the saddle. But Timur was returning, and his weapon must be forged in the heat of impossible difficulties. Unlucky the Afghan in the path of those raids who thought to defend himself and retaliate! To avenge the death of one of Baber's marauding generals who had been struck down by an arrow, eighty men of the

Hazaras were smoked out of a cave where they had taken refuge and were massacred.

By dint of his repeated absences the Prince-Errant made a valuable discovery, namely, that his enemies were less dangerous than his friends. At Kabul, the office of chief minister was filled by the influential Baki Jaganiani. Although his master knew him for a sordid, greedy, perfidious man, corrupt in his private life and short-sighted in his public policies, yet he was obliged to walk softly where that minister was concerned. For Baki's position was extremely powerful ; he was head of the former partisans of his brother, Khosrau Shah, men who composed the largest part of Baber's army. Undismayed by his brother's fate, Baki Jaganiani had rallied to the side of the young prince, in the hope of receiving a large official plum at his hands.

Having won an important position, he became overweening in his insolence. He ordered a drum to be beaten outside his door—the usual sign of royalty ; Baber said nothing. He contrived a plot that failed ; still Baber said nothing. He sought to obtrude himself upon public notice by handing in his resignation after every rebuff in council, then recalling it as soon as it was offered.

At last he dared to remind Baber that the latter had promised to forgive his faults "till nine times." Immediately he received a list of eleven important grievances.

The hint was fairly obvious, as was also Baber's increased strength. Baki Jaganiani had to bow before the indomitable will, and left for India with his family and goods—encountering on the way a notable

Afghan bandit who took his treasure and hewed off his head.

That removal was a great comfort to Baber. For the power of Asiatic despots was never so great as has been imagined. Far from being unlimited, it was hedged about by a multitude of conflicting forces. A prince's power was never any greater than the prince himself. A despot was the leader of a pack of wolves; he held his place only as long as his teeth were sharp. The essence of his authority was not absolutism but the absence of laws; violence was the inescapable result. Despotism was a synonym not for omnipotence but rather for perpetual warfare.

Scarcely had Baber freed himself of his redoubtable minister when a new care waited upon him. His brother Jahangir, persistently faithful to him after their reconciliation at Akhsai, had even more recently proved his fidelity by denouncing Baki's conspiracy. But then he fell under the influence of two Mongols whom he had taken into his service, and changed his manner abruptly. Without warning he dropped the reins of his government at Ghazni and retired among the Mongol tribes of the west to prepare an uprising.

Baber forestalled him easily enough, however, when the revolt came to a head. At the moment he found himself with his house in order at last. He had got rid of his doubtful soldiers, of his treacherous minister, and of his two brothers—one being at Badakshan and the other in the steppes brewing his rebellion. And he had done all this without spilling blood.

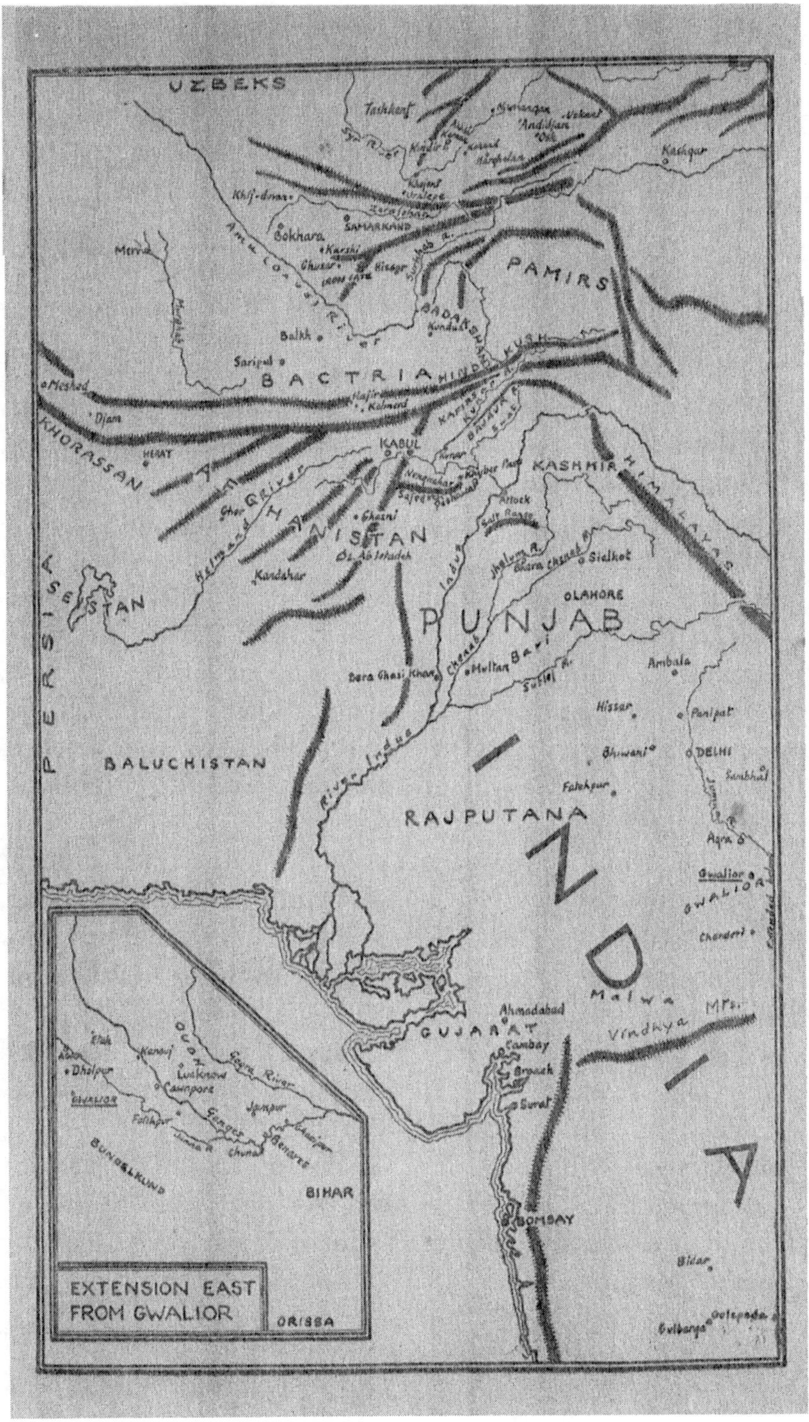
UZBEKS
Tashkent
Andijan
Kashgar
SAMARKAND
Bokhara
Karshi
Hissar
Merv
PAMIRS
BADAKSHAN
Kunduz
Balkh
BACTRIA
HINDU KUSH
Meshed
KHORASSAN
HERAT
KABUL
KASHMIR
HIMALAYAS
Ghazni
Kandahar
SEISTAN
PERSIA
Attock
Sialkot
LAHORE
PUNJAB
Dera Ghazi Khan
Multan
Ambala
Hissar
Panipat
DELHI
BALUCHISTAN
RAJPUTANA
INDIA
Agra
Gwalior
GWALIOR
Chanderi
Malwa
Vindhya Mts.
Ahmadabad
GUJARAT
Cambay
Broach
Surat
BOMBAY
Bidar
Gulbarga
OUDH
Kanauj
Lucknow
Cawnpore
Dholpur
Jaunpur
Benares
Chunar
BUNDELKUND
BIHAR
ORISSA
EXTENSION EAST
FROM GWALIOR

CHAPTER SEVEN

HERAT, PEARL OF KHORASSAN

SHAIBANI, that formidable rival, still wore the laurels of success. The puissance of the Khan of the Uzbeks waxed till its proportions became profoundly disturbing. He had occupied Khiva after a siege of six months and was now sitting in strength before Balkh. The Amu River, which for a while had seemed a sufficient moat to defend the last fragments of the Timurid empire, had been crossed from the west as well as from the east ; Herat was menaced.

The old Padishah, Hussayn Baikara, shook off the torpor of approaching death and called to the defence of his city all his vassals, his sons and the princes of his house.

Baber would have been the last man to refuse such an invitation. To strike at Shaibani, his own particular enemy—that was his *delenda est Carthago*. The campaign that he anticipated seemed to offer in addition the chance of undoing the schemes of Jahangir.

He therefore answered Hussayn's message by setting out toward Heart immediately. The instant he came over the northern watershed of the Hindu Kush, the Mongol tribes declared for him, leaving Jahangir naked to the winds. At once that turncoat found reasons for resuming the old fidelities ; he rejoined his amiable brother, who allowed him in his presence once more. The latter pursued his way over the flanks of the mountains, never descending to the plains, because they were infested with Uzbek horsemen. And on the second day of October, 1506, on the banks of the Murghab, he was met by a courier from the sons of the Padishah.

Their father had died even before Baber had left Kabul.

The passing of Hussayn Baikara marked the close of the Tamerlane chapter in Iran. Thirty-seven years before, on a halcyon day of ringing battle songs and arms, he had won his realm in high conflict, the most beautiful part of the empire, as lovely as a queen, stretched upon its glorious couch from the Caspian Sea to the Indian Ocean. Hussayn was a man of rare vigour and presence, broad of shoulder, with the chest of a lion and the waist of a greyhound, and the best sword of that dynasty of swordsmen.

He prided himself no less upon his skill in poetry and had composed a "divan" that had been honoured by more than one celebrated writer. He was the true figure of a Grand Monarch. But like others of that lineage of heaven, peace had softened his fibre and had invited intricate pleasures. Mighty in song, he was mighty also in the companion exercises of the cup: invariably sober in the morning, he drank without measure the instant midday prayers had been said. Indifferent to religion, he was scarcely able to distinguish between heresy and orthodoxy and turned to the latter quite by chance, when policy forced him to it.

The customary fasting never appealed to him; consequently he was afflicted with gout and rheumatism in his later years. But even that was construed as a virtue by the incorrigible *bon vivant*; it enabled him to renounce without regret the genuflections and prostrations of the devout Mussulman.

His temperament, beyond that, was a mixture of the fiery with the playful, even the childish at times: he had an exalted passion for cock-fighting, enjoyed watching the rams fight, and wore extravagant robes of green and red silk, with a tall feather planted in the folds of a carelessly wound turban.

For the legitimate wives that chance had given him he had no liking whatever. One of them, the mother of his eldest son, was a virago, jealous and unbearable; he finally won peace by divorcing her, and she had died of chagrin. Another was repudiated because instead of being in the saddle on the day of a certain battle she remained in her litter, persuaded that she had nothing to fear from the enemy since it was her own brother. Hussayn divorced her because no intelligent woman could have believed so implicitly in the brothers of that period. A third, Khadijeh Begum, concubine raised to the rank of a lady, was always hatching plots so stupid that the least page in the palace knew all about them. Hare-brained, she could not stand contradiction; she encouraged squabbles beween her children and their father; and she had the habit of poisoning people whose conversation she found distasteful. To Hussayn, wives were a plague.

Every ill has its cure, goes the Turkish proverb.

Hussayn found balm in numerous mistresses: of his fourteen sons only three were legitimate. Baber disapproved of all this disorder and debauchery in the royal family. And when, eight years after the death of the father, not a single one of his children was alive, the prince saw evidence of the punishment of God.

From the indolence of Hussayn Baikara in his decline sprang the fortune of Uzbek and Turkoman to the north-east and west. They had enriched themselves by paring down his kingdom. And his heirs were not the sort to repair the damage. "They were," says Baber, "pleasant young men who had all the virtues that ornament the relations of man with man; but they were total strangers to the arts of war and of government." Unfortunately, amiable conversation was not an accomplishment with which to impress those rough fellows, the Uzbeks and Turkomans.

To make the plight worse, the succession in those days was ordered by strange rules: the new sovereign had to be chosen from among the princes that were present at the actual death of their father. On this occasion only two were found eligible – Badi-uz-zeman, the eldest, who normally would have gained the crown had not the other, Musafer Hussayn, been the son of the dangerous Khadijeh.

The chieftains added a slip to the Gordian knot by making both of the sons kings, each with his minister and his chief of police.

And the stage was then perfectly set for anything but order and peace. The immediate result was stagnation of military activity. The army sent against the Uzbek near Murghab remained idle for months, arms stacked. Receiving no help, the town of Balkh fell into the possession of the enemy, and Shaibani went home at the approach of winter absolutely unmolested.

Hussayn Baikara's exit made Baber's presence at Herat the more necessary. When he had heard the courier's words, he pressed on, ready to give to the sons the aid he had promised to the father. He was made very welcome when he arrived at their capital. The cadet galloped out to meet him beyond the gates, and gave him escort into the city. The eldest alone remained in his palace until Baber should present himself.

Observing the usual etiquette, the visiting prince knelt upon entering the presence-chamber, then hurried towards Badi-uz-zeman, who, on his side, advanced with calculated slowness. At that, the former became impatient with the prescribed forms; he was about to take one step more than the rules called for when a punctilious lord caught him by the belt and halted him.

Baber's natural and pleasant spontaneity was constantly overriding ceremony. But he never allowed himself, or others, to forget the deference due to him. When, during their second interview, Badi-uz-zeman showed less respect toward him than on the occasion of their first, the proud young prince pointed out that though he was not a greybeard, no one present was of higher birth than he, that he had twice occupied the throne of Samarkand and had sustained innumerable combats against the enemies of their house. It was therefore unseemly to curtail in any way the honours due to him. Badi-uz-zeman apologized.

He was, as a matter of fact, badly in need of a watchdog. Would his young cousin be pleased to take up winter quarters near him ? Baber found objections to the idea : it would not be prudent to remain too long so far away from Kabul. The province was as yet like a very restive horse unbroken to its new master ; and if anything should happen there, to return would require a month by the mountain passes—provided they were not blocked with snow—and six weeks by way of the plains.

Nevertheless, at the redoubled insistence of princes so august, he deemed it polite to yield, and consented to remain. It may well have been that he allowed himself to be persuaded largely because of his youthful desire to see celebrated Herat, whose splendours were proclaimed second to none—the world over.

The converging point of all the great highways into India, Herat boasted magnificence as well as importance. It was in the form of a huge rectangle set broadly in the centre of a plain amid walled vineyards, and was bounded by ramparts nine miles in extent that gave entrance at five gates to the city of miracles. If one came from Samarkand or Kandahar, one marked the town a great way off in the valley because of what seemed to be a single blazing jewel set in the outer wall. For the portals were of carved and polished sandalwood, studded with silver-headed bolts, inset with copper shields and clamped with burnished steel. So that when the sun shone upon them, to a traveller coming out of the distant mountains, Herat was a single great ray sped from those bright gates.

If he entered by the road from Irak, he came at once into the quarter of the tradesmen and craftsmen, where the squat clay hutches covered the ground like pebbles in the bed of a mountain stream. The web of buildings there lay tangled like the weaving of the wool-spinner. The narrow ways straggled about among the flat roofs, past the arched gates of the caravanserais in whose courtyards mules and camels were laden with their bales, past the shuttle and clack of a rug-maker's shop or the tapping of chisel on ivory, leading at last to the bazaar—the *charsu*—built by the great Hussayn Mirza.

There he might rub against the savage Khiljis, the sheep-raising Durani, or the Yusafzais, come to buy arms, or the Hazaras, come to rob. He might be jostled by the vendor calling mulberries, or the importunate diamond merchant from Bundelkund and Golconda, or the trader who would sell him—at a loss—a Bokhara rug worth ten diamonds. There he might buy the delicious wild rhubarb of Kabul, the bananas of Ispahan, the oranges of Damascus. There were stalls full of damascened swords and of bows insert with jade and tourmaline; illuminated books from the hands of skilled calligraphists whose prices were as extravagant as those of the Bokhara rug-seller; silks of Herat next to silks of China; drinking cups hollowed from coral of Araby; unbored pearls; obscene golden images from Hindustan . . . and girls from everywhere, ready to be turned before experienced eyes.

But the real glories of the city greeted the traveller as he went northward. There the royal Hussayn Mirza had spent most prodigally of the gold of his imagination and of his realm. The southern and western quarters might be of clay, brick or rough stone; but here the buildings were of marble or of brick faced with porcelain tiles that shimmered luminously, so that the walls stood in the air like vertical plains of light against a dark sky. Blue, white, and pale green, the palaces and mosques rose a glittering hundred feet toward the sky. Here was the platform of cream-coloured marble, unadorned save by ramps, of the tomb of Shah Mansur; the black slab and arch that stretched over Ansari's grave; the golden domes and minars of the Mosalla, built at the command of Hussayn; and, across a tiny stream, the nine jet sarcophagi, shaded by domes of gold and lapis lazuli, that did honour to Gohar Shadi, the Beautiful.

To the east was the incomparable mosque erected by the order of Hussayn, the Masjid Jamah, blue porcelain without, and rank upon rank of columns within, four hundred and forty of them, that sustained a vaulting of gleaming mosaics over an area which was nearly half a mile square. Its windows numbered one hundred and thirty, and its azure and gold cupolas, four hundred and eight. This magnificence was to the glory of the One God and of the mighty Ghyas-ud-Din, who slept beneath the unimaginable crown of light in a sepulchre decorated by the hand of Ali Shir.

Near at hand the visitor found also the garden of Ali Shir, the pleasure-walks given by him to the public, the Raven Garden, the White Palace built by the Irak Gate, the Pleasure House, the great reservoir, the porcelain fountains and water channels, Ali Shir's Palace, his mosque, his colleges and his hospitals.

But beyond these, and second only to the Masjid Jamah, was the palace of Hussayn Mirza Baikara, glowing like a cluster of precious stones on a slight hill in the north-eastern quarter of the city. The red-and-yellow flowers called the *ur-shavan* hid the ground where it stood. Yet in its splendour it outdid the miracles of Nature. When the Padishah erected it, he brought marble from Jaipur and red sandstone from Fatehpur. Jasper came to it from the Punjab, China sent its jade and crystals, Tibet its turquoise, and Arabia its coral and cornelian. He ordered amethyst from his own province and lapis from Badakshan for the domes. And he sent to Kanauj for inlay workers, and to Shiraz for the calligraphists who should draw the inscriptions.

Close by he laid out gardens that he found worthy of the palace, and in the centre of them he had stretched a pavilion of scarlet velvet that required eighty poles to uphold it. Its silken hangings were fragrant with musk, and the carpet stretching from it to the durbar in the palace was scented with vapours from burning amber.

The proverb ran, "Khorassan is the oyster shell of the world, and Herat is its pearl."

Blue, white, and pale green upon the dusty floor of the plain beneath a clear sky, to a traveller coming out of the mountains Herat glittered with delicately coloured fire, as a pool of water is shaken into iridescence under bright wind and sun.

In Herat, then, the fascinated Baber remained. And under the eyes of those finished gentlemen, his cousins, the feasting began ; and it continued almost without intermission until he left. It was as lavish as it was gay. The dishes were of chased gold and silver, the viands were delicate and various. Once, when Baber, not knowing how to cut it, dared not touch a roast goose, Badi-uz-zeman carved for him, "doing it with exquisite address."

The most renowned singers and musicians performed in a way to justify their golden fame ; for those of Herat surpassed in the exactness of their pitch and in the finesse und subtlety of their harmonies. Several noblemen danced gracefully ; one of them giving undeniable proof of art in a step of his own invention.

The tides of wine flowed hugely, but Baber had not yet learned the practice. His intimate friends always hid from him to do their drinking. When at Kabul, they would quaff behind doors that were securely tied shut. Here they drank behind their broad sleeves, or they profited by the moments when their master's head was turned. For Baber neither drank nor wished his retainers to drink. And Badi-uz-zeman pressed him in vain.

One day, nevertheless, the thought came to him that he would never find so excellent an occasion for initiating himself into the pleasure of wine as in

Herat, where there was every resource of luxury and voluptuousness. He decided to "venture on a voyage into the unknown enchantments of drunkenness"—drunkenness because these men knew no middle ground; they saw in wine only exaltation, confusion, delirium.

Baber was a guest of the younger brother that day. He suddenly recalled that since he had previously refused the cup of the elder, to drink now would be to offer an affront to him. Etiquette gave his sobriety a longer life by five years.

During his first week he paid a visit to the princesses royal, all of whom were assembled for the occasion in the mausoleum of Hussayn Baikara. He knelt before every one of the windows of the defunct sovereign and, rising, took their two hands in his own, after the Turkish fashion. He dined with Khadijeh, and spent the night at the house of Pajendah, whom he tenderly called his "little mother."

Returning to her a few days later, he met in her entourage a young girl, named Maasuma. She immediately fell in love with this handsome prince; and it was arranged that she should accompany him back to Kabul.

But before that, he must explore the city, like a veritable tourist. He went everywhere, storing up in his mind the strange beauties he saw. Perhaps there was mingled with his pleasure the premonition that his cousins did not possess the charms to hold the strumpet Fortune at their side forever; some day she might accept his own advances and confer upon him this jewel, Herat.

For the moment he was content to revel in the miracles of architecture that stood about him, all the more glorious because they sprang out of the mire of filthy streets. Like a tourist, he knew precisely what he meant to see next: gardens, palaces, mosques, colleges, tombs, houses of charity, hospitals, baths, kiosks, markets, fountains, bridges, monumental gates —everything was fixed in his memory, even the grave of the holy Abdullah Ansari, called the Laundry, because, according to the poet, "the rain of the Divine Clemency there washes and makes spotless the souls of men."

But Iran had monuments more enduring than its structures of stone and porcelain, its symmetrical gardens, or its work in gold and in velvet. Its great and imperishable glory was its galaxy of writers.

One of Baber's first cares had been to pay his homage at the tomb of Nur-ud-Din Abd-ur-Raham, the poet above all other poets, "too great to need Praise"—Jami.

Persian literature had never shown so brilliantly as under Timur and his immediate successors. Within a century and a half one might number a hundred and eighty-eight writers of the first class and at least a dozen great poets. That this efflorescence had developed under Turkish domination was a phenomenon the more remarkable when one considers that the national dynasty of the Safavids, although it later won back nearly all of the lost kingdom and restored the glories and traditions of a famous Persia, nevertheless presided over a sadly decadent literature.

For under the later dynasty Iran was divided between two powerful enemies, the Safavids and the Uzbeks, the Shiites and the Sunnites.* The two sects differed in name, but they were alike in being bigoted, fanatical, narrow and cruel.

The Timurids before them had on the contrary been liberal in spirit, great lovers of the arts and of letters and infinitely interested in the play of the mind. Nowhere in the world and at no time, either during the Italian Renaissance or under the Valois of France, has history known princes of such natural good taste, so sincere and unaffected in the pleasures of the spirit. Let the political condition of the country be what it might, they were always generous patrons of the creative arts. A victory in arms was merely useful, but a poem by Jami was the occasion for a triumph. Changeable, unsteady, torn to shreds though their realm was, they never forgot that their chief glory came from the pen and the brush. They might be greedy, but they never stinted the gold they spent on their artists.

To be sure, the most of their intellectual activity was in writing that was purely literary. Science had little place ; and philosophy was up to the neck in the quicksands of theology or was clothed in the immaterial mantle of mysticism. But, under that garment of obscurity, what hardihood of thought and manner was concealed ! Sheltered there, the poets celebrated love and all earthly joys, which they thinly disguised as divine love and the celestial felicities.

And so Metaphor grew to gigantic proportions. It

* See Appendix B.

was to them the reflection of the unseen Reality ; the bridge toward the Ideal ; and they willingly lingered upon it. More and more they became attached to form, to skilful address, artificial refinements and ingenious turns of phrase. And to this particular cycle of writers, Persian literature owes its reputation for studied elegance, emphasis and excessive figures of speech.

It was a mode that came westward after a time. In England it became the euphuism of Elizabethans ; in Spain is was the *estilo culto* of Gongora ; in Italy, the *concetti* of Marini ; and in France the witticism of the *précieuse*.

Baber laughed heartily at a certain noble poetaster who, not content with the Springs, Streams, Torrents and Floods of Tears that lovers have spilled since the beginning of the world, had written : "The whirlwind of their sighs has shattered the skies ! The torrent of their tears has drowned the habitable earth."

The greater poets, like Jami, preserve the energetic conciseness of the old masters. But in this period even the writers of prose, even the historians, joyously cultivated the Garden of Puns, and bathed in the swollen streams of Metaphor. Consider for example this sober passage from Khandamir, the court historiographer of Hussayn Baikara :

"At the happy birth of the glorious monarch, the light of the star of his horoscope illumined the inhabited fourth of the globe. And when the bright moon saw the glitter of his beauty, ornament of the earth, she ceased to borrow her rays from the sun."

Or, again, somewhat more familiarly : "The tree of

enmity springs from the soil of discord; and, watered every day by the gardener of destiny, its fruits ripen until they fall upon the field of unhappiness."

In certain respects the century of the Persian Timurids was as brilliant in art as in letter; the century that came after, though better known in Europe, was only its feeble, long-drawn-out death. In particular, the books and manuscripts of the period maintained a standard that the rest of the world has never equalled, in excellence of paper, in beauty of characters, and in sumptuous and perfect bindings, and in their illustrations, where the splendid harmony of colours disputes the prize with sureness and ease of design. Iran of the Timurids was past master of the microscopic arts: its carved ivory and engraved steel are unrivalled.

The glory of its carpets has never been touched, even remotely. In that essential article of Oriental furnishing, the supreme was attained. The artists translated superbly the dream of their national poetry in their dyed threads. And the imagination in a sort of vertigo follows this poetic dream through the repetition of intricate motifs into a semblance of infinity. The startling nuances, growing miraculously one out of another, the sinuous grace of the forms, all the magnificent variety of this perishable world that ends so suddenly, leaving its trace within the threaded frame of a divine unity—therein the Persians wove their poetry better than ever man has written it.

In his Memoirs Baber presents a gallery of literary and artistic portraits that makes his work an important document of contemporaneous civilization. We can set down but a few of the picturesque figures scattered through his pages.

One meets, for example, the Sheik-ul-Islam: pious judge, inflexible ascetic, a profound metaphysician, so fond of chess that when he met two men capable of matching his skill, he would play with one and detain the other as a reserve by clinging to the skirt of his robe.

Another Sheik-ul-Islam talked of nothing but strategy and the military art, and was so obsessed by the subject that he narrowly escaped insanity.

And there is a great poet, Binai, who was once taunted with his ignorance of music; he thereupon studied the art during the whole of one winter, and when spring blossomed, so also did he, as one of the best musicians of the era.

The famous Ali Shir, his confrère, was a powerful minister and a great popular favourite. Binai detested him, for Ali Shir was commended here and praised there. Ali Shir excelled in the arts of the boudoir and the garden as in that of politics. Whatever trick or accomplishment there was that was worth while, Ali Shir mastered it! ... Binai lost all patience. Once, when about to set out on a journey, he sent to the bazaar to place an order with Ali Shir for a saddle—for his ass! The occurrence passed into a proverb.

We learn, too, that the poet Saifi of Bokhara was a quarrelsome drunkard whose fist was mighty when it had the wine cup in it—and when it had not; and that Palevan Muhammad, the poet and incomparable musician, was also the champion wrestler of his day.

Baber prises most highly the caligraphers, the painters, the players of flute, guitar and lute. He appreciated their talent, but he also believed in keeping them in their place. He recounts how his enemy, Shaibani Khan, rapped a musician vigorously on the head because he performed on the lute with such poor technique and feeling.

"And that," he added, "was, by my faith, the best thing he ever did in his life! These light-weight artists who give themselves such ponderous airs deserve corresponding punishment!"

CHAPTER EIGHT

TREASON AT KABUL

BABER, like the Emperor Nero, was guilty of playing while a city came down about his ears. Seven months had elapsed since he had left Kabul: and his past experience had taught him that strange things may happen in the absence of a prince. Awakened sense of caution, and the fact that his cousins could not furnish him with adequate winter quarters, made him turn again toward his own city.

On the twenty-third of December he set out eastward, travelling in leisurely stages until all of his men should have joined him. Two or three precious days were wasted in that fashion; some few of the soldiers left Herat, reluctantly, and overtook the main body; some found the city too comfortable, and so changed patrons.

And then . . . there was no question of Baber's impatience. Suddenly he was all for haste. Followed or not, instead of turning the mountains by Kandahar to the south, he held to his eastward course and plunged into the granite terrors of the Hindu Kush; for he resolved to go to Kabul by the straightest course. He had marched far up the pass, beyond the scant timberline, when snow began falling so heavily that all traces of his route were obliterated. The blizzard forced him to retreat many precious miles before he could find wood for fires against the deadly cold.

The snowfall became heavier and more blinding. His men huddled about their fires while a detachment went out in hopeless search of a guide. After four days they returned to their half-frozen comrades without one. Baber put himself in the hands of God and went forward.

On one side of him was snow that might give way suddenly to send horse and man spinning down upon the frozen torrents ; on the other side was snow that might at any moment drop from the cliffs above to bury man and horse or sweep them off to abrupt death. . . He went on at the rate of four miles a day.

His road ran somewhere under the great drifts, somewhere through the mad swirl and vortex of the winter. It seemed to sway with the wind at every perilous ledge ; it was nothing but a white menace that smothered and blinded and froze the eyeballs : it did not exist. Every other moment it had to be made.

Baber and his intimates took turns in heading the column and breaking trail. Each one would struggle ahead for sixty yards, up to his waist in the snow he was packing down, almost hurled into it by the violent wind. A riderless horse followed for the same distance, plunging up to the stirrups in the drifts. Then man and steed would be replaced by the next pair. And over the road thus beaten down the troop rode without dismounting.

"It was not a time to stand on ceremony," says Baber. "Under such circumstances, the man of courage simply has to offer himself for hard service." Therein the prince showed that his tremendous physical strength was not the greatest of his virtues: he knew men; he knew that in the hour of crisis the command is nothing and the example is everything.

One afternoon, darkness came earlier than usual. More fiercely than ever the storm roared down the pass, cutting off the daylight above the steel-grey cliffs. The troop halted before a small cave where the curve of unseen rock gave them some shelter. They remained all night on their horses while Death breathed through their mail and laid hands of ice on their helmets.

But when they would have Baber take shelter in the cave, he was angry. He would not sleep safe and warm while his men were out fighting the storm.

"Had I done that," he says, "I would have proved myself heartless toward my comrades in arms. I preferred to suffer what they suffered. For it is said, 'To die with one's friends is as good as a wedding feast.'"

With a shovel he scooped out a hole in the snow, squatted down in the slight screen it provided against the wind, and awoke the next morning with a foot of snow over his head, and his ears frozen.

Now the sky no longer spat peril. Without a halt they pushed on through the Pass of Zerrin and out on to the southern slopes of the range. The bitter cold froze the feet and hands of many a lord. Baber saw plainly that he had not chosen the best route; no one had ever before conquered the mountains under such conditions. But the extraordinary youth merely congratulated himself upon the presence of the snow, which had allowed him to climb escarpments which without it would have been impassable.

Obviously, adversity is a blessing . . . to those who know how to use it. The prince was an optimist and a very active one.

On the following day they came to the village of Yeka-Ulang, where the exhausted beasts had shelter and fodder, and the no less exhausted men found warm rooms and an abundance of fat mutton. They remained there for twenty-four hours, grateful for the rest and the comfort. Then Baber ordered the horses to be saddled, and the force rode out afresh, this time up the northern slopes toward Bamian, and thence down into the plain of Kabul.

In the first village they passed, Baber heard news that made him drive spurs into his horse and brought his company to the gallop : Khan Mirza, son of his uncle Mahmud Mirza and governor of Kabul, was laying siege to the citadel ; the rest of Kabul was in his hands already.

As cousin derived from the same paternal and maternal grandfathers, Khan Mirza had elected to accompany Baber in his exodus from Farghana. Later, when the Prince-Errant had come to Kabul, this cousin had been joined by his mother, Baber's aunt, and by his grandmother, a most dangerous mischief-maker, Shah Begum. The latter had great influence among the Mongols at court as a widow of their former Khan, Yunas, and mother of his two successors, Mahmud and Ahmed.

Once more family relations aped the fashion of the century: when Baber went to Herat the two women plotted to exchange cousin for cousin at Kabul. Spreading the rumour that Baber had been made prisoner during his visit, they won over the greater part of the Mongols, notably, Muhammad Hussayn Doghlat. This uncle of Baber has figured in his nephew's history before. After the defeat of the two Khans at Farghana, he took refuge with Shaibani.

That shrewd leader, however, saw no advantage in the presence of any chieftain who might conceivably influence the thirty thousand Mongols of his own army. He tolerated no rivals in its affection. Through a common friend he had advised Muhammad Hussayn that he had too much regard for his life not to urge him to flee. The warning came to Muhammad at midday; three hours later, he was thirty-five miles away.

He had then sought out Baber and had received a cordial welcome at his hands : his nephew had made him viceroy of the province during his absence in Herat. By way of showing his gratitude, Muhammad had now proclaimed Khan Mirza lord of Kabul. The city had been docile; but a few faithful nobles had shut themselves within the central fort, to hold it for the legitimate prince. It was the delay caused by their obstinacy that permitted Baber to arrive in time.

When he learned of Muhammad's treachery, Baber pushed on by forced marches with a select body of horsemen. He communicated secretly with the besieged, then fell without warning upon the rebels in the suburbs of the town. The street-fighting, he says, was remarkably effective, probably because his murderous sword had a part in it. The traitors, caught in the rear by a sortie of the loyal garrison, were finally routed, and Kabul's lord entered into his good city overwhelmed by the tributes of affection and devotion that are the reward of the successful man.

Immediately, without stopping to put off his armour, he paid a visit to the breeders of all this trouble. At his sudden entrance the two princesses were thrown into confusion, and burst out with excuses. Baber treated them with extreme courtesy, addressing not a single word of reproach to them.

"I have travelled a long way," he said, "and am very tired." Then he fell asleep on the breast of Shah Begum.

Meanwhile, Muhammad Hussayn, traitor-in-chief, by way of hiding, had rolled himself up in a rug and concealed himself in a closet in the house. The quaking man was discoverd by the servants, who brought him to Baber. Expecting to be killed, he was pardoned and given his freedom. But instead of using it wisely, the foolish man returned once more to Shaibani.

His former lord listened to Hussayn's complaints about Baber, judged him a turncoat without a head worth keeping, and commanded that it be removed. It was.

"The reward he deserved!" commented Baber, and wrote a disdainful and haughty epitaph for the fool:

Leave to destiny the man who wrongs you;
Better than yourself will it avenge you.

As for Khan Mirza, he had left Kabul just before

the street-fighting began. Pursued and captured, he also was received kindly by the man he had thought to wrong. As he was dragged into Baber's presence, "Approach! Embrace me!" said the enemy. And Mirza was so overcome with emotion that he collapsed before the prince could reach his side. They sat down to table. And victor placed vanquished at his right hand and offered him a cup of sherbet, tasting it first so that Khan Mirza might not fear treachery.

The uprising being fresh in the people's minds, the prince advised his cousin to retire to Herat until Kabul should quiet down. A little later, he ordered him to take over the rights which were his in Badakshan. Another enemy had been defeated by kindness.

At this point in his Memoirs, Baber tells of the clemency with which he treated the various members of his mother's family, and of the black ingratitude with which they repaid him. Then he adds:

"I write all this, not in the spirit of accusation, but in the spirit of truth. I do not mean to speak my own praises. I desire merely to put down things as they have occurred. In these Memoirs I have determined to say nothing that is not rigorously exact. I have written all that can be said, both of merit and of fault, concerning those who have been friends or strangers. I hope that my readers will be indulgent toward me, and that those who hear this book spoken of will not judge me too severely."

Spring came. The hurts inflicted by man's perfidy still smarted. For consolation, he went to his gardens in the mountains near the city. It was the season when this place was the loveliest on earth. There on the green slopes he walked and rode and flew his falcon. The world was fresh, and the varieties of tulips infinite. In the scented air of the blazing gardens he composed the ghazal which begins:

My poor wounded heart is the bud of a rose
Folded as yet in dark crimson petals.
Breathed upon a thousand times by tender spring,
May it not burst at last into full flower?

CHAPTER NINE

THE SCEPTRE OF TIMUR

A PHILOSOPHER'S wounds may heal amid quiet gardens that mirror his dreams. But a man of action assuages the sting of disappointment by vigorous movement. Baber was host to the two moods in succession: he sang his tristful lyrics; then, these finished, sprang into the saddle.

After the spring of melancholy, he undertook a raid in the south against the Khiljis Afghans, in order to replenish his purse. The take in sheep alone was so enormous that as his own share—a fifth of the total—he wrote down sixteen thousand in his records. After having thrown up the usual pyramid of owners' skulls as a monument to regal rights, he returned home, driving such a vast herd before him that the sentinels on Kabul walls marked the dust clouds as the approach of some overwhelming invader. And when he came to the gates, the people flocked to greet him with such a welcome as meets the mooring of an argosy.

Properly to celebrate the occasion, a great hunt was arranged in the plains and the neighbouring foot-hills. A thousand servants and four thousand soldiers stationed themselves at various posts, and at a given signal spread out in a great circle and beat toward its centre. Wolves, bear, the small antlered deer, the hare, the panther, were driven in to the point where death awaited them in the person of Baber with his unerring bow.

Suddenly the horns were sounded and the beaters called in. Grave news had came from Herat, and a messenger awaited the prince at his palace.

Closeted with the lord of Kabul, the messenger told how Shaibani had set out in April with a huge army of over forty thousand, bent on the capture of Herat, and how the two princes, when they had heard of his coming, had drawn up their forces a few miles to the east of the city, near their summer palace of Baba Khaki. They had come, he said, to oppose the Uzbeks. But the partisans of the co-rulers were a quarrelsome lot, and a battle of words had divided the army into two camps. Discord had paralyzed further action.

Muhammad Berenduk, Musafer's minister, had proposed a sensible scheme : his prince would defend the city while Badi-uz-zeman held the slopes of the mountains, where his vizier, Zul Nun, had a considerable following. Shaibani would not dare attack him there, nor would he venture upon Herat with such a force threatening his left flank. Thus Herat would be saved.

But Zul Nun was as rapacious as he was brave, and would not leave the city to his rivals, lest they should bar his return. Thus the time had flown, while uncertainty and inertia clogged the only plan of campaign. No measure of safety had been taken; no organization of the troops, not even the drilling of them had been attempted.

Demoralization ensued. So, when Shaibani arrived,

his adversaries were unable to re-form in battle line and close with him. All was distracted confusion. The panic-stricken warriors deserted the field to a man—and Timurid power had vanished like a dream!

Only Zul Nun faced the enemy—as foolhardy as he had been foolish. A holy man had flattered him with the prediction that he would defeat the Uzbeks and win the surname of The Lion of God as had the Kalif Ali. He believed the prophecy. Knotting a towel about his neck in token of his vow, he threw himself upon the enemy with the hundred men of his guard.

The ranks opened to engulf the tiny force, then closed. This forlorn hope and its crack-brained leader were never again seen alive.

By the time that Zul Nun had thus paid his worldly obligations, the unworthy descendants of the great Timur were back in Herat, where they spent the night. At dawn they fled; and three days later, May 27th, 1507, the Uzbeks marched into possession of their city, their mothers, wives, sisters and children.

Shaibani knew how to play the conqueror. He distributed the women of the royal family among his friends, who held them for the exaction of heavy ransoms. His second move was one of incomparable malice : all the poets of the city, including Ali Shir, he delivered to the mercies of their great rival Binai, and his good colleagues were duly washed in lye and hung out to dry.

Baber draws an amusing sketch of Shaibani at Herat, giving lessons in exegesis to the most learned doctors of the Law, retouching with a pen the designs of the great painters of the age, ordering a ribald couplet of his own composition to be delivered from the high tribune of the mosque and then levying a collection upon the congregation for having listened to it. Baber's animosity rather obscured his judgment. Shaibani, though a Uzbek, was highly cultivated, versed in the Persian and the Arabic tongues, a very good poet in Turkish, and a strict follower of his faith, acquitting himself faithfully of the five daily prayers and the reading of the Sacred Book. As a rule, he treated writers and artists liberally, and carried his library with him on all his campaigns.

Prince Badi-uz-zeman had escaped from his pursuers. His brother Musafer and another son of Hussayn Baikara had been overtaken at Meshed ; only their heads were brought to Shaibani.

Such was the news that recalled Baber from the hunt. Thus had ended the dynasty of Tamerlane in Central Asia ; or at least, it was now represented by only one sovereign prince—himself.

The next step was logical ; and, though his own state was a small one, he did not hesitate : at once he assumed the rôle of Head of the family, and in that quality reclaimed the lordship over the Arghuns, who had been for a long time the masters of Kandahar under the nominal authority of the Padishah. They had sought help of him in the first moment of their fright over the Uzbek triumph. He responded by marching toward their city at the head of two thousand soldiers.

When he arrived, however, he found that the Arghuns had regained their courage. Their chief wrote a very uncivil note to him, affixing his seal to the back of the paper and in the middle of the page. It was a formulary employed by amirs in writing to others of non-royal rank. Baber immediately put the city under a state of siege.

Food was scarce in the neigbhourhood, so that a thousand of his men were off on marauding parties when the Arghuns came out of their gates and offered battle. Only a thousand were left him. But he says that for the first time in his career he had a well-drilled and disciplined army. Every company knew in advance what it had to do. Every division had its special name. The right and the left wings of the combined force were called *barongar* and *jungar*, while the corresponding wings of the centre were given Turkish names that meant "right hand" and "left hand." And the two wings of his own guard, the nucleus of the centre, had Turkish names equivalent to our "right flank" and "left flank."

The fight was a lively one, with Baber outnumbered four to one. "But," he remarks simply, "everything succeeded to our hearts' content, thanks to the help of God." The battle was won by the thousand efficient men ; the city at once capitulated, and Baber's Turks won rich booty of camels and mules, fabrics and velvet pavilions, and chests of wrought metals, clothing and money.

"Let not my lord delay on account of this, however," advised Kassim Beg, the Nestor of Baber's councillors. The advice was sound, for scarcely had the prince turned his heel upon Kandahar when Shaibani came up and occupied the plundered city.

Flight before Shaibani's thousands was not a problem ; it was a necessity. The only question was, where ? Badakshan and Hindustan were suggested, Baber swinging the scales in favour of the latter, so that once again the young prince stood on the edge of his later conquests. After making provision for the safeguard of Kabul he began the journey eastward in September of 1507. But destiny, in guise of the Uzbek Khan, was so pressing that he went *à l'improviste*, without a single plan for the future.

And then, having launched him, Fortune drew him back until a better occasion. At the ford of the Kunar he learned of the unexpected retreat of the terrible Shaibani, who had gone to disperse a rebel attack upon the castle near Herat where he had placed his family.

Apparently unmoved by the extraordinary ebb and flow of his fortunes, Baber re-entered Kabul, gave thanks to God, and assumed the title of Padishah. That meant that he regarded himself as Timur's lawful successor, suzerain of the House of Timur and even of the Mongols—in brief, Kha Khan or sole heir of Genghis. His claim was somewhat academic, since without an empire the crown was bare of jewels. But empty honour though it might be, men were certain to arise who would dispute it with the new Padishah.

Not at the moment, however. The winter passed tranquilly. At the end of it he celebrated by a magnificent feast the birth of his first son, Humayun. The mother of the child, whom he had taken to himself in Herat two years before, remained his favourite until the end. Neither he nor any one else mentions her antecedents. With affectionate simplicity her husband always called her *Maham*, My Moon, My Beauty.

Presently the snows melted, and with springtime fresh activities were afoot. Our over-refined civilization has disregarded this law of nature. But less civilized man, nearer to the earth, feels the need of shaking the ice out of his blood after the torpor of winter ; and for him there is no better way of doing it, none more pleasant and lucrative, than by war, revolt, brigandage.

In the new Padishah's following very many men were close to the soil. His service was filled with Mongols who were born pillagers and therefore intolerant of a prince who stood for order. They cared little for his new title, reckoning a single sword at a higher price than sixteen unsupported quarterings. They flared up in open mutiny in an attempt to replace on the throne the Timurid Abd-ur-Razzak, whom Baber had dispossessed. Probably the Arghuns had a hand in the affair on the side of the ousted claimant.

Following the very general rule under such circumstances, defections multiplied among the officers of the prince. The rank and file deserted to the Timurid relative by the hundreds every day until Baber found himself reduced to five hundred men. He owed his safety then to his intrepidity, his superb swordsmanship and his genius for outmanoeuvring his enemy. A battle was forward at once—one of his greatest, according to Muhammad Haidar—in which he slew five Turkish champions of the insurgents in single fight, and with his compact five hundred destroyed their army. . . Its unlucky head, his cousin, was pardoned—to be executed a little later after a second injudicious uprising.

And here at the beginning of his account of the Mongol revolt, in the very middle of a phrase, the text of the Memoirs breaks off, not to recommence until twelve years later, in January, 1519. It has been supposed (without any particular reason) that this hiatus is deliberate. It is much more likely to have been the result of an accident to the original text. For the manuscript went through many misadventures. The author himself tells how one day a sudden storm came up and swept through the room where he was writing, scattering his papers everywhere, so that only with the greatest difficulty was he able to find all the rain-soaked pages. Later, his son Humayun carried his father's Memoirs with him through an exile of fourteen years (1541-1555) without any copy other than the original.

Baber first took notes on events as they happened and then reworked those notes. Up to this point, May, 1508, the Memoirs are an example of finished writing. When they recommence in 1519, they are nothing more than a journal, carefully done, no doubt, but not yet in final form. Death, then, must have interrupted his editing somewhere within the limits of the existing lacuna.

The loss is the more deplorable in that it concerned the period of his conquest of India ; and not only his intimate life but the general history of all Asia seems to have been reflected in it. For just at this time a new power arose and spread over the western part of Timur's empire, as Shaibani's rule had over the east. Power of an unprecedented kind, it was not from the sword of a tribal chieftain or a man of royal descent. It came from a priest's son, the head of a monastic congregation, a sect of Islam.

CHAPTER TEN

A FIREBRAND OF ALLAH

ISLAM was all gentleness at its birth. Had its practice supported its theory, it would have been the parent of love rather than of destruction.

For its writ finds no place for a man of military, political, or clerical ambitions. Properly speaking, the religion even lacks priests ; its believers are all equal, and brothers, before God. There is no intermediary between the creature and his Creator. But out of the mass of the simple faithful arise men of a singular piety called *sufis* who disdain the literal interpretation of the sacred word and exalt their hearts with an elaborate and mystical interpretation, moving through the Love of God from solitude and renunciation into Knowledge and Truth, to end at last in complete absorption into the Divine Essence – which is Nirvana under another name.

Actually, the doctrine is that of Buddhism, with its atheism transformed into a Muhammadan theism by a refinement of language. The mystics produced by the cult hold that all religions are but the varying instruments whereby man attains to Reality ; that everything in the sensible world—objects, beings and acts—arises out of the divine Substance, in which it is but a transitory accident ; and that in Unity, good and evil are one.

Discord within the sect sprang chiefly from the consideration of two problems : the reconciliation of the foregoing conceptions with the idea of the existence of a God and of His attributes ; and the question of personal responsibility and free will. Certain of them, such as the Ismaïlites and Mutazilites, believed that one cannot say that God exists and that He is eternal and omnipotent, because Existence is not, apart from Him, and Eternity and Omnipotence are one with Him. Others, such as the Muzdarites and the Wamiyehs, said that since God is the creator of all things, He is the author of all human actions, and that therefore actions are without moral consequence to the individual.

But the ordinary believer was not touched by theological hair-splitting. The religion maintained its power over him by means of the *sufis.* These men, aloof from the crowd, inspired it with reverence because of their unworldliness, and with terror because of their supernatural gifts, whereby the Mussulman recognized the Chosen of Allah.

The manifestation of those gifts meant in reality only such puerile wonders and impositions as have always brought the commonalty to the feet of a wonder-worker : extraordinary dreams that foretell the future, second-sight, thought transference, the finding of hidden objects, the ability to appear and disappear at will, trances, immunity against poison, the control of objects at a distance, the answering of difficult questions, sermons to animals, prolonged fasting, mysterious punishment of offences, and finally—more important than all the rest—abnormal sexual vigour.

The saints thus marked by the divine seal fathered disciples around them. Communities more or less widespread were formed whose members were called *fakirs* in Arabic, *dervishes* in Persian. They were bound by special rules, committing them to penitential tortures, violent devotional exercises, and passive obedience to their superiors.

In the thirteenth century one of these venerable *sufis* called Safyi-ud-Din, a poet, claimed descent, through the seventh Imam, from Ali, the son-in-law of the Prophet. He established a brotherhood at Ardabil in the north-west of Persia, and gave its rule over to his sons when he died. For a century and a half the congregation held to its sanctity while it increased its worldly strength, so that by the fifteenth century it numbered ten thousand adherents. The climax of temporal power had been reached, apparently, when the fourth descendant of the founder allied himself with the Turkoman dynasty of the White Sheep by marrying the sister of Uzzun Hassan.

But after five children had been born in the second generation to signalize the alliance, the nervous Turkoman lord destroyed the symbols of unity by massacring all of the offspring.

All, that is, save one, a mighty infant, Ismaïl, whose nurse fled with the year-old babe into the forests of Guilan. In the year 1500 Ismaïl came out of them with seven companions to re-instate the dignity of his line.

He rallied about him the faithful of the brotherhood. He met and killed the king of Shirvan, against whom his father had been fighting when he was slain ; he captured Baku, defeated the lord of the Turkomans, and was enthroned in his place at the amazing city of Tabriz in 1501. He was then fourteen years of age. During the seven years that followed he shattered the last strength of the White Sheep dynasty, he reduced to silence the dozen princes who were squabbling over Persia, and he won Baghdad. So that at twenty-one he was reigning over a ·kingdom eight hundred thousand square miles in area.

There is in all this an astonishing similarity to the histories of the greatest men of that era—Baber, Shaibani, and Hussayn Baikara. All of them had begun their careers by losing everything and going into exile. All, save Shaibani, who developed tardily, gave proof in infancy of their immense powers; so that the strength of their armies cannot of itself explain their precocious success. One had to admit that in spite of their tender ages their genius was irresistible.

Three Venetian travellers—Caterino Zeno, Angiolello, and an unknown—have left vivid portraits of the youngest of them, not the least extraordinary, Ismaïl. By their evidence he was extremely handsome, of noble bearing, graceful as a girl and as light on his feet as a deer, with sand-coloured hair, broad shoulders, and delicate hands that yet could shoot an arrow two hundred yards straight to its mark. He had the look, the quick determination, the condescension, and the ferocious turn of mind of a conqueror. His soldiers adored him.

His domains extended east to Shaibani's frontiers. He was ostensibly at peace with the hot head Shaibani when the latter closed his eyes to a foray into his neighbour's kingdom. Ismaïl sent a complaint to him. Shaibani insolently told him to return to the trade of his fathers, and dispatched a pilgrim's staff and a dervish's bowl to emphasize the invitation.

Ismaïl retaliated with these verses:

Boast not of your dead father !
It is a hungry dog that gnaws such bones !

adding that battle would decide between them, and that if Shaibani would not accept the challenge he could occupy his leisure time with the gift accompanying the letter. The gift was a distaff.

The Uzbek would have found spinning infinitely safer. Ismaïl's attack found him in evil case, when he had just returned from a severe test against the Hazara bandits that had exhausted and demoralized his army. He attempted a retreat, but Ismaïl drew up with him at Merv. Genius and superior forces combined to scatter the weary Turks like driven leaves.

Closely pursued by the victors, Shaibani and a few of his men galloped into a cattle-pound a short distance from the field, looking for escape. They could find no exit from the enclosure, and the enemy were already riding through the gate. In desperation Shaibani set his horse at the high stockade ; the horse failed to clear, and its rider's skull was crushed in the fall.

Ismaïl had the corpse cut into small pieces and distributed to the several parts of his empire. A hand was solemnly conveyed to the rebel prince of the Mazandarans ; when it was unwrapped before him the prince immediately had a seizure. To the Sultan at Constantinople, Bayazid II, was sent another such souvenir stuffed with straw—the head. Ismaïl himself kept the skull and had it mounted in gold to serve his as a drinking-cup.

Following up his victory, he entered Herat and ordered the prayers to be read from the pulpit of the mosque according to the Shiite creed. The Persian declared that the safety of his own old life was an nothing compared with the sanctity of the True body. He was hewed in pieces then and there.

Ismaïl then called upon the Sheik-ul-Islam to chain the first three Kalifs. He refused. So Ismaïl shot him down with an arrow from his own bow and had his body chained to a great log and burned in the market-place.

Unlike Baber, Ismaïl believed the True Faith to be always necessary to the happiness of man ; by bloody persecution he imposed Shiism upon the empire. That empire had been doubled in size by his victory over Shaibani, and now covered an area of 1,600,000 square miles, stretching from the Euphrates to Kandahar and from the Caucasus to the Indian Ocean. In content it was nearly the old empire of the Sassanid dynasty which had ruled Persia from 226 to 652. The ancient Persian monarchy thus seemed to be restored after eight and a half centuries of Arab, Turkish and Mongol dominion.

But empires do not consist entirely in geographical boundaries. In this instance there was a vast difference between the old and the new. In the former, the power and the glory had been the expression of a national spirit ; in the latter it was nothing more than the triumph of a religious sect. In the new body politic there was not the slightest community of race, tradition or language. Some large provinces had a non-Iranian population that spoke only Turkish or Arabic. At the very court of the Safavids the Turkish tongue continued in use for a long time, the nucleus of their power having been the clans of that race.

Ismaïl's empire, in other words, was a Chinese puzzle of hostile elements. Only the force and terror of fanaticism held it together. The land flamed with religious wars. The Persians hated Sunnites,* and so they killed the Ottoman and Uzbek Turks; and these retaliated by murdering the Persians because they were Shiites. Shiites they had not always been, however; the great Safyi-ud-Din had professed Sunnite doctrines.

Ismaïl, the first to change the family creed, was wise enough to use Iranian traditions as well as the sword in his evangelizing campaigns. He turned for help, therefore, to that buttress of all tyrannical traditions—the society of learned doctors. And they, imbued with Persian mythology, discovered many ancient conceptions which they now introduced into Islam under the aegis of the Shiite lord.

One was of especial importance. It was the idea of a divine right of kings, in the exact sense of the phrase; that is to-day, kings were divine by reason of their celestial origin, which had been transmitted from their first ancestor, the Son of God, to all his descendants from father to son. By analogy—and their world was plunged into blood because of this—they found that only Ali, the fourth Kalif, son-in-law

* See Appendix B, 3.

and adopted son of the Prophet, and his direct descendants, could claim the title of Kalif or Imam; that these alone were qualified to command the army of believers; and that the first three Kalifs had been usurpers, and so had all their successors.

In reality, Ali's sacred line had ended with its twelfth representative, in 870, after poison and the knife had removed all collaterals.

That objection, however, did not disconcert the managers of this theological revolution. To meet it they discovered a second truth—which is to be found in nearly all national mythologies: the myth of the hero-god, believed dead, who remains hidden for his hundreds of years, to reappear eventually like the sun at morning or like the blades of grass in the spring. That is to say, the last Imam, Master of the Hour, who is now closed within a secret grotto, will return triumphantly at the end of the ages to establish justice —in favour of the Shiites.

For that reason the Safavids, though they claimed lineal descent from Ali, never took the title of King of Kings, but rather called themselves humbly "the dogs at the gate of Ali." They were lieutenants reigning in the stead of the hidden Imam—for whom they kept a horse saddled in their stables, night and day.

Such were the elements of the new Persian monarchy, and such was the groundwork for the religious revolutions that moved in equal strides with it. The two factors changed the face of Baber's world and exercised a dominant influence over his own fortunes.

CHAPTER ELEVEN

FICKLE FORTUNE AND TWO FAITHFUL MEN

IN mid-December of 1510, when the passes were blocked with snow, a messenger arrived at Kabul, swaying on his horse from exhaustion, with both feet frozen. The letter that he delivered brought Baber to the saddle; and when he had ridden a day's journey, it set him face to face at once with a recent guest of his and with a rarer thing—fidelity.

At the age of twenty-four Saïd Khan was not the least singular of those romantic figures created by destiny with so free a hand in that exuberant epoch. When only sixteen he had' been wounded in battle at Akhsai at the side of his father, Ahmed Khan, and then had been captured by the Uzbeks. After spending twelve months in prison, he was given a post at the court of Shaibani, who seemed to favour the young man. But eventually, in his customary manner, the lord suggested to Saïd that he would probably be much safer elsewhere.

Saïd fled to his uncle, Mahmud Khan. The effeminacy of his relative disgusted him. Impatient for action, he escaped, routed the troops sent to retake him, and won through to the Mongol country with a shoulder splintered by an arrow.

There he indulged in plot and counterplot, sometimes with and sometimes against his brothers, but always against his uncle. He was badly beaten by his eldest brother at Kulja, and again was barely able to save himself by flight.

With fifty men, his servants and his wives, he endured two weeks of forced marching across the mountains and valleys of the Tien-Shan before he could find a place of refuge for his family. Then, accompanied by one man, he rode away to a party of Kirghiz who were camped three days' distant, to propose that the two bands should travel together.

They treated him with extreme insolence, detained his companion, and thrust him out of camp to ride back alone. He learned from a traveller that during his absence his men, thinking that he did not intend to return, had quarrelled and broken with one another.

He now had no choice in the life he might lead. A man deserted in that barren country was a vagabond; he had to sleep on the ground and live off the chase. Every day he would climb to a look-out and gaze anxiously over the horizon after the habit of the Mongols. If it was free of men, he would ride from noon until midnight.

Late one evening he came upon a group of his own men, with their wives, busy putting up their tents. Jaded and at the very end of his endurance, he removed his boots and lay down to sleep; but his men begged him to keep his boots on; he would be captured if they were attacked in the night. Saïd compromised by sleeping with one off and one on.

A sudden clamour awoke him in the middle of the

night. The tents were blazing around him. With one foot bare he sprang up to face a detachment of horsemen from Kashgar that had been sent out to clear the mountains of enemies, brigands and vagrants.

Most of the women and the horses were captured by the attacking party; but Saïd and his men managed to escape. They rode all day and hid when dark came in ravines and forests, watching anxiously at dawn for the slightest hint of danger; then they held a formal council: it was agreed that the situation was hopeless. Implacable enemies awaited them in the valley. But they could keep to the mountains no longer, for their quivers were empty, and the entire band had but a single arrow among them.

Surrender or perish! They chose to surrender, to the enemy that was nearer and the less dangerous—the Khan of the Uzbeks.

Saïd Khan gave himself up at Andijan; its governor fastened his hands to his neck by means of a wooden stock and sent him to Jani Beg, Shaibani's lieutenant in Farghana. By good luck Jani Beg was in excellent humour and had been so ever since his horse had thrown nim a few months before. He had fallen on his head and was deranged mentally. The Beg generously gave Saïd his freedom, and sent him back to Andijan. There the governor made great cheer for his guest; and the two men celebrated the happy occasion in cups of wine that were filled and emptied through the whole of a day and a night.

Meanwhile Jani Beg, somewhat recovered, repented of his magnanimity and dispatched a man to Andijan with orders to have the desperate Mongol executed.

"The lord Jani is mad !" cried the governor. "I have no man about me so deadly as that !"

"He sits there by your side," pointed out the messenger.

The governor was furious : "How dare you contradict me, who am well known for my eminent services to my lord ?" and he had the messenger put in stocks outside the city gates.

The next day, Saïd parted from his newly won friend, in a beggar's habit and accompanied by several notable personages disguised as merchants and domestics. He turned south and crossed the mountains by nearly the same route that the fugitive Baber had travelled several years before, and came at last to Kabul, in desperate need, he and his six men almost naked. Baber gave his young cousin a warm and friendly welcome and bestowed upon him one of the best fiefs of his principality.

During the time of his stay in Kabul, which lasted from November, 1508, to December, 1510, Saïd Khan laid up many a happy memory. "The days that I spent in that city are the happiest and most lighthearted I have ever known. I lived for nearly two years at the court of its estimable prince in a succession of pleasures and diversions. I was never melancholy there save when I had drunk heavily the night before. And my only annoyance arose from the caprices of a beautiful mistress."

Now, Saïd Khan had gone to Kunduz. And it was there that Baber came after the messenger had ridden to him in mid-December. Saïd Khan was the recent guest—and that rarer thing—the man of fidelity.

The messenger had been sent by Khan Mirza, the new prince of Badakshan, to announce the defeat and death of Shaibani and place himself at the disposition of the Padishah in case he wished to retake his ancestral Samarkand from the Uzbeks.

With the letter crumpled in his fist Baber was on his horse and away to Kunduz, meaning to march upon Samarkand at the first opportunity. He found himself heading for a hornets' nests. Twenty thousand Mongols were camped there, the former soldiers of his uncles Mahmud and Ahmed who had shared in the defeat of Shaibani. Now they were free, without master and without control, as dangerous as the shifting ballast in a vessel. Baber could not entertain with any pleasure the thought of facing them with an army numbering only five thousand. Secure in their strength, they offered to place Saïd Khan in Baber's shoes.

But the man would not betray his cousin's hospitality and affectionate confidence. He refused to listen to any Mongol plots ; more than that, he warned Baber of them, telling him that for the sake of their friendship the two had better part.

About that time appeared a chief of the tribe, a former retainer of the Uzbek captain, who had taken advantage of the confusion that followed his lord's death to drive the Uzbeks out of Farghana. He came to do homage to Baber for the state. But Baber, touched by the generosity of Saïd Khan, gave the fief to his friend. The chief was furious. Baber, however, had merely exercised his prerogatives as Padishah. In the Memoirs he dismisses the incident with "I made him Khan." For he was ruler, in name at least, of the western Mongols just as the emperors at Pekin were lords of the eastern Mongols. He had another reason, too, for the award : he was glad to honour a faithful man.

Baber's arrival strengthened Khan Mirza's position which had been very unsteady. He had proclaimed his rights in Badakshan ; but several parties were engaged in ignoring them when the prince came. There was Abu-Bekr of Kashgar, master of the hill-districts to the east ; and the Uzbeks, camped in the plain along the Amu River ; Razi-ud-Din, the Ismaïlite adventurer, posted between the two ; and finally Zobeir, the most influential of the native country chiefs. Under such circumstances the province, according to Muhammad Haidar, had the total value of a small loaf of bread. He doubtless knew, for when the future historian was still a youth he had taken refuge there from Shaibani.

Khan Mirza himself had undergone all the disgrace and reverses that Fate could inflict. He had been defeated by Abu-Bekr, who carried off his grandmother and left her to perish in a dungeon ; he had been imprisoned by Zobeir ; repeatedly he had been the victim of ferocious Ismaïlites* under Razi-ud-Din.

The murder of the latter by some of his own men was a slight comfort to Baber's harassed lieutenant ; but not until the prince arrived from Kabul was he secure from attack.

Baber Padishah had thrown himself into the Samar-

* See Appendix B, 3.

kand enterprise without any plan, being of the opinion Fortune favours the brave and energetic. Now the Uzbeks recovered something of their former balance. They elected as Khan the eldest member of their royal family—Kutshunji, an uncle of Shaibani. He remained at home in Turkestan, and distributed his doubtful acquisitions among relatives : Tashkent went to his own son, Suyunjuk ; Samarkand was given to Timur, a son of Shaibani ; Bokhara to Obaïd Allah, Shaibani's nephew ; and Andijan to Jani Beg. The result was a confederation of considerable power. Inspiration alone could not defeat it.

Baber was champing the bit at Kunduz because of it, when he received an embassage from Shah Ismaïl. The Shah was pleased to give back to him his sister Khansadeh, wife of Uzbek Khan, who had been captured on the field of Merv. The princess returned to her brother accompanied by signal honours. She had been given a brilliant escort, a large body of servants, and all of her possessions. Baber rode out to meet her ; but they had not seen each other for ten years, and there was no recognition on either side.

Yet he loved her, and so was touched by the respect that Ismaïl had paid her. But he was not blind to the fact that the courtesy was nothing more than a polite invitation to form an alliance.

It was inevitable. Baber could do nothing by himself, and Ismaïl was so thickly embroiled in his struggle with the redoubtable Ottoman power in the west that he could not put down the Uzbeks in the east without help. The Padishah sent his cousi

Khan Mirza, to the Shah, charged officially with presents, thanks and congratulations, but privately with instructions to treat with him upon the subject of the alliance.

Ismaïl dictated leonine terms. Badakshan and Hissar were given to Khan Mirza ; and to Baber was given whatever he could win in Transoxiana with the aid of his great ally and under his authority. Baber, in short, was to be his vice-regent in the east.

After receiving the Persian reinforcements that his cousin brought back with him, Baber took the offensive and advanced clear to the boundary of the Amu River. But the Uzbeks, having nothing to fear now from the personal intervention of the Shah, struck with all their force at him and at Saïd Khan in Farghana. Their manifest superiority compelled the Padishah to retire to the south until snug in the gorges of the Hindu Kush.

He took up a strong position and awaited the enemy.

The attack was almost overwhelming. But toward evening, all their charges having failed, the tribesmen withdrew to camp for the night near the river in the bottom of the valley. Then Baber ordered a counter-attack, and his men galloped down the slope into the confused rearguard of the Uzbeks, which broke and fled. He pursued them all night and all the next day, until the last of them had been driven to the pass known as the Iron Gate. The entire province of Hissar was the fruit of his victory.

Immediately, of course, the mountain tribes flocked around him. Ismaïl, whose terms he had accepted, sent him a strong reinforcement under an older relative of his, Ahmed Sultan Safyi. The combined armies now totalled sixty thousand. The two generals marched directly upon Bokhara, ignoring Karshi *en route*, where the reserve troops of the Uzbeks lay, under the command of Obaïd Allah. The latter had not expected such a manoeuvre ; he was caught unawares. But in an attempt to defeat the trick played upon him, he hurried out with his army, determined to be the first in at Bokhara. It was a battle of speed ; and Baber and the Persians won the race. They occupied the city, and Obaïd Allah had to retire into Turkestan along with the garrisons of Samarkand and Tashkent.

Baber went on. Once over the Amu River he was received with joy by the towns and villages ; and for the third time, in October, 1511, less than ten months after leaving Kabul, he made a triumphal entry into Samarkand. The pomp of the occasion had never before been equalled. The street and the bazaars were hung with gold brocade, and the people shouted and praised God.

But not for long. Even as their beloved prince rode through the narrow streets they saw Persians in his train. They saw that the army was full of the detested heretics. They suddenly found out that Baber, their favourite, was making common cause with the evil Shiites ! Scowls and silence now greeted him.

Baber indeed tried to disengage himself from the awkward predicament. He had sent back most of the Persian auxiliaries after the taking of Bokhara ; now he treated the ambassador of Ismaïl with a certain coolness. Whereupon the envoy complained to the Shah, saying that this vice-regent did not appear inclined to fulfil his obligations, now that he was in Samarkand once more. Ismaïl dryly reminded his ally of the terms of the pact, and made a gesture toward his large army.

The prince had to give in. He needed the Persian arms desperately, and for him to remain politically a Sunnite, no matter how lukewarm, meant that he would lose them without winning over the Uzbeks, who were his enemies in any case. Lip-worship was all he would ever give to the Persian creed. He had been raised in the Sunnite doctrines, and he remained faithful to them throughout his private life, attesting later the sincerity of his beliefs by writing a religious poem of the most exacting orthodoxy. But Samarkand was his dearest ambition. And as Henry of Navarre considered Paris well worth a mass, so did Baber four score years before him hold his city well worth the forswearing of half a dozen dead Kalifs.

He therefore repeated the prayers for Friday in the name of Shah Ismaïl and the twelve Imams. And he adopted for himself and his troops the detested coiffure of the Red Heads (Kyzyl Bash)—the conical scarlet turban of twelve points with a long red banderole streaming behind. And thus he kept Persia as an ally. But, caught between the devil and the sea, he alienated his own subjects.

The customary peace of winter at an end, Baber made trial of the strength of his position. It could not have been weaker. The native Sunnites refused to serve in his army, the heretical Persians had already left it and returned home. As a result, the new master could not in a crisis rely upon more than five or six hundred faithful men. His weakness and the grumblings in orthodox Samarkand encouraged the Uzbeks to action. They took the road and marched upon Bokhara by way of the desert, hoping in that manner to scatter their opponent's strength over his entire western border.

Burning with his usual fire, Baber refused all conservative advice. He sprang after them, overtook them near their goal, and engaged with them on the spot. At first it looked as though he would win a victory ; the Uzbeks were slaughtered in great numbers. But the tide of battle turned against his tiny force, and it was crushed under sheer weight of men.

With such as could get free of the press the Padishah fled back to Samarkand. The leaving of his city was becoming a habit. He halted there long enough to collect his family and possessions, then rode out through his beloved Turquoise Gate—for the last time. With hard riding his handful of men gained Hissar and took refuge behind its wall before the Uzbeks could reach them.

Suddenly, without any warning, the sun of Baber's fortune wore a pleasant face. A large force of Persians was marching to his aid. The Uzbeks discreetly retired. And in October the lord Baber joined with his allies at the Iron Gate, placing himself under the command of the Persian general, Najm Sani, the Shah's own minister of finance. Acting in concert, they captured the villages of Ghuzar and Karshi, where the entire population, in spite of the Timurid's wishes, was massacred, even to the women and the unweaned babes.

The enemy Uzbeks now found themselves threatened in Bokhara. They fell back to the small town of Khij-duvan on the edge of the great desert, and entrenched themselves behind the hedges and in the ditches at the roadside and behind the garden walls of the oasis. The Persians came up, superbly confident in their numbers, their horsemen riding in close array. From the very first charge, however, the carnage wrought by the Uzbek arrows was tremendous. It was scarcely necessary for the Uzbeks to come from behind their defences. And Muhammad Haidar could record with satisfaction, "Then was sent to hell the heretic Najm Sani, and the bloody swords of Karshi were avenged."

Shah Ismaïl's method of promoting his officers after such a battle appeals by reason of its great simplicity. He had all the lieutenants of the dead general executed, acting on the theory that a dead officer cannot repeat his blunder.

As for Baber, he had been placed in reserve on the day of the fight, perhaps had been left with very few troops. At any rate, he was already disgusted with the inhuman conduct and arrogance of his allies. . . . For he withdrew from the battle almost without striking a blow. At the Persian court his action was condemned as treason; even twenty years later his son Humayun, while an exile there, had to endure many reproaches on his father's account.

No one is less respected by the professional soldier than a defeated commander. When Baber returned to the stronghold of Hissar, his Mongols were only too ready to betray him. As he slept one night in his camp, they revolted suddenly. He escaped to the citadel of the town, alone and in his nightclothes. His faithful garrison there could protect him; but it was powerless to retake the city from the insurgents. So the harassed prince of Kabul escaped from it under cover of darkness and fled south of the river, abandoning Hissar to the pillage of his Mongols, who ransacked it from cellar to attic.

After them came famine and pest. Under the heavy snows that fell that winter a tragic misery desolated the city and its countryside. Thousands of women and children were sold as slaves. . . The Mongols by their very excesses had deprived themselves of money, goods, food, and the people to produce those necessaries. They were defenceless against the attacks of the Uzbeks, who in due time exterminated them.

And Baber, as he rode alone toward Kunduz through the falling snows and obscured starlight, knew that he, who had lost Samarkand and Bokhara for ever, had now lost Hissar.

Once again it was made clear to him how frail and precarious a thing was power. His political organizations had crumbled away as quickly as he had raised them. No cement held them together; they were composed of individual self-centred particles as ready to disintegrate as a swarm of mayflies—as sand in a storm!

The prestige of his name could rally to his standard

those who found it convenient, advantageous; but obligation and loyalty were words to provoke savage laughter. Timur, dead and gone to earth, was impotent to aid his ambitious young descendant.

According to our European notions, Baber should have returned to his estates in Kabul after his leadership had been discredited, his army scattered. He remained two whole years in Kunduz, like a bird on a swaying branch, with Khan Mirza, his kinsman and vassal, awaiting a more fortunate occasion that would enable him to recover his lost empire. . . The nomadic spirit persists in even the most cultivated Turk.

For, unlike the Venetians and Florentines, or the French and English, the Turk had never developed a common interest with the rest of his people, no sentiment of nationality that might lead him to make war and peace, as leader of a unit. with some other unit. The exact contrary: an Oriental never spoke of war as a national affair. To him a province was nothing but a field to be charged over by regiments, or a source of revenue at the disposal of a prince who used it for his own purposes, abandoning it at pleasure or necessity and attaching no more significance to it than to any castle he had built. He was on a par with, as mercenary as, the European feudal baron of the Middle Ages. His castle, which was personal to him, meant more than the land of his birth or any other land.

Hence Baber, being destitute, stayed away from Kabul. We know little about his sojourn at Kunduz and Kishm in the years 1513 and 1514. But we know that he waited vainly for an inviting opportunity.

The Uzbeks held fast to the Transoxiana—his one-time holdings north of the Amu. The Kazaks menaced them here and there, but were too content with their steppes to make a formidable bid for the effeminate cities.

Said Khan still ruled at Farghana ; but he could be of little use to his benefactor, for he knew that he himself bestrode a restive horse that might at any moment throw him. By 1514 his position had become untenable, and with all his Mongol retainers he migrated eastward to the other side of the mountains. There he conquered all of Eastern Turkestan between Kashgar and Turfan, Dzungaria and Kashmir, and governed his new empire gloriously until death overtook him in 1533.

Shah Ismaïl, once disappointed by the prince, was not inclined to renew relations with him. In addition, he was threatened in the west by the powerful Osmanlis. There he remained, aloof from Baber, and on guard. And there he suffered a disastrous overthrow at Tabriz, in August of 1514.

With his defeat the light of Baber's hope was extinguished. At the end of the year he re-entered Kabul after an absence of four years, and took again the government from the faithful hands of his younger brother, Nasir Mirza, to whom he had confided it when he left. Barring a brief period of disaffection following the raid into India, Nasir Mirza had proved a regent to be trusted.

This brother's fidelity was so rare that it was the

admiration of his age. The less generous have cynically suggested that it may have been due to absence of ambition—product of the cup. At any rate, he found death there. His immoderate taste for wine carried Nasir Mirza off the following year from his little fief at Ghazni, still faithful, still calm, in the flower of his age and of Baber's gratitude.

CHAPTER TWELVE

BABER LOOKS AT INDIA

THE Padishah's third attempt upon Samarkand had not been altogether without profit. He was now the overlord of Badakshan, where Khan Mirza acknowledged his authority. And he had so impressed the Bactrians that their governor paid him the tribute that should have gone to Shah Ismaïl.

His territory was about equal in area to the British Isles. Though not large, it could be made the nucleus of a larger state, thought Baber. He must solidify it.

The historian of Akbar's reign, Abd-ul-Fazl, says that the prince on his return to Kabul was divinely inspired to achieve the conquest of India. The divine inspiration, however, took the form of the Persian disaster of Tabriz, which stripped from him the last hope of reigning over the Central Asia of his fathers. Obviously he must turn to another field, though he appears not to have known where it was to be found.

If he had confined himself at the outset to the northern side of the Amu River, it was because there he had friends, allies, and a knowledge of the country. India was to him all but *terra incognita*. And he was not disposed to fly his hawk at an eagle in a strange country when he might have safe hunting in lands familiar to him.

At present, there was work to be done that required

immediate attention. He held a very uncertain hand over the Afghans ; and even the people of his own race were restless. The death of the gentle Nasir Mirza had unkennelled a host of rebels, Turks as well as Mongols, who were disputing as to the succession.

Among them were men who should have been the most faithful of vassals, who had spent their entire lives in Baber's service, who had received special favours at his hands. But Oriental sovereigns could not keep friends save by continual conquests and by the general glut offered by huge forays. Timur's heir had about him a full share of dispossessed princes and impoverished lords whose appetite it passed his immediate power to satiate. He was forced on pain of death and extermination to enlarge his borders. He must win an empire, not for himself but for his lords.

But, first of all, he must prepare the soil, acquire new friends, and make new connections. He must blunt the edge of hostile swords with intrigue.

After putting down the main revolt and exiling most of the turbulent vassals, Baber undertook a series of punitive expeditions for the purpose of ridding himself of the more intractable elements among his people the Hazaras, the Aymaks, and the Afghans. His procedure was always the same: he moved with a small body of cavalry by secret and forced marches, fell upon the encampments or villages by surprise, killed or dispersed the men and added the women and cattle to his train. Thus his revenues were assured for some time to come, and bridgandage in the plains and mountains was not so common a pest.

Kandahar occupied the prince's mind constantly. That city in the hands of the puissant family of the Arghuns disturbed him. He had chased out Shah Shoujaa Begg once before. Shaibani had restored him. And on the death of the latter the Arghun had gone to pay his respects to Shah Ismaïl—who clapped him into a dungeon near Herat. One of his slaves disguised as a baker had distributed drugged cakes among the jailors, and his master had escaped.

Once back in Kandahar, he foresaw an attack by Baber and prepared for it. So did Baber. A severe illness, however, tied the prince's hands just as he was about to crush the stubborn fellow, and he had to content himself with a vague declaration of submission from the Shah.

But Shoujaa understood that he was being given no more than a breathing spell and that his adversary would return to his design. Still keeping his city in a state of preparedness, he went down into India to hew himself out a spare province there along the lower course of the Indus between Multan and the sea. There he meant to retire if Baber attacked again.

In the four years that followed Baber may be said to have had no history. But he led a very active life, of which his journal of 1519 gives a very precise idea. He was almost continually on the road at the head of a cavalcade, receiving homage—which generally took the form of a horse richly caparisoned, in return for which he bestowed a robe of honour—paying visits to faithful friends in order to stimulate their zeal, punishing the wayward, pillaging the treacherous and cutting off heads.

When he had garnered enough of these grisly trophies, he would build a monument of them on some conspicuous hill. It was not cruelty on his part ; it was merely an Asiatic method of advertising the advantage of obedience. It was the most effective means of maintaining order and peace.

Pillage was another thing. It was natural to him ; it was an expression of the man and of the necessity of his times. He speaks frankly of it, without any disguise and without any cynicism. His raids were made where rice and wheat were to be had ; very simply, they were shopping trips.

"We resolved," he writes in one place, "that since grain was plentiful in Hashnagar it was expedient to lead a raid against the Afghans there."

In case of submission, pillage was replaced by a tax ; and Baber fixed the amount. One way or another, he collected his state revenues.

These expeditions were not only for business ; they gave him a great amount of pleasure. Along his road he shot tiger, antelope, fallow deer, and duck ; and, when he went into India, the rhinoceros and elephant. Sometimes he flew his falcon ; but he did not greatly enjoy this sport, being unlike most of his lords, who counted the death of a son as nothing beside the loss of a peregrine falcon.

He found delight, too, in travel for its own sake. He journeyed on horse, by boat, on rafts ; he spent many hours in fishing, and in visiting local curiosities. He dug reservoirs, examined water-wheels, constructed dams, built terraces. Admiring all beauties of the countryside, he resigned and planted gardens in spots that particularly pleased him ; and once he razed the tomb of a heretic that was disfiguring an especially enchanting view.

He loved Nature ; not in the fashion of the romantics, who prefer the picturesque and the savage, but in the manner of the true voluptuary, for its grace and its delicacy, the freshness of its springs, the sweetness of its green shadows and the brightness and perfume of its flowers. It gave him a sensuous thrill even to pass by the Garden of Fidelity that he had caused to be planted on the left bank of the Kabul river across from Adinapur.

"The borders were of plain clover. And the trees glowed beneath their rich foliage with every imaginable tint. The pomegranates flashed red, and the orange-trees charged the palette with the curious shade of their unripe fruit."

He would turn back to look at an apple-tree "which had borne so heavily that on a branch there was place for only five or six leaves. No painter, regardless of his skill, could have shown the wonder of it."

He was ravished by the beauty of the gardens of Peshawar. "Yellow and purple flowers covered the earth. In one place nothing could be seen but great yellow blossoms ; in another, the ground seemed to have been sown with bits of glittering silver. I seated myself on a little hill that looked on the garden, and let my gaze rest upon the lovely terraces. Over the flanks of the hills ran six long flower beds, regularly laid out and displaying ranks of astonishing beauty, wherein yellow alternated with red. And as far as the eye could reach it discovered similar terraces."

Perhaps these gardens borrowed some of their magic from the enchanted paste, hashish (*maajun*), that Baber always ate before visiting them. Since his return from Samarkand he had taken up the habit of the strange drug and had associated it even with wine—contrary to the refined practices of both cults, and in spite of the contempt that the devotees of one showed for those of the other.

Everything that gave him an agreeable impression served as a pretext for calling for his gold drinking-cups : a ride through the woods, a sailing trip down the river, a lovely view, the gathering of the harvest, a meeting with some loyal vassal. He would assemble his friends and talk of art, literature and philosophy. They recited verses, they played on the guitar or the lute, they sang songs, and finished with a heavy drinking bout.

The parties were held about every other day, in the afternoon or at night ; and sometimes they recommenced at dawn. If the day were fair, they drank out of doors. If it rained, they shut themselves up in the palace, and Baber would teach one of his friends a charm against sudden showers.

He was a jolly companion, utterly lacking in affectation and something of a wag. One day there was brought to him a colocynth, an intensely bitter fruit and a powerful cathartic. He told one of his lords who was not familiar with it that it was a choice melon from Hindustan, and enjoyed hugely the gourmand's subsequent discomfiture.

On another day, the notion took him to drink his wine on the banks of a canal. "Such and such a lady," they told him, "would like to drink in your company, sire." "I have never seen a woman partake of wine," answered the prince, surprised ; "nevertheless, go find her." The party was charming and lasted until the sun came up ; and the lady drank Baber under the table.

Upon another occasion, he saw an ambassador going by *en grand équipage*. He stopped him, saying: "Forget that you are on a mission of state. Save your official demeanour for to-morrow's audience, and come and drink with us!"

The sequel reveals more of the prince's character. The ambassador was an abstainer. And Baber, though he often railed at his kind, never made them violate their scruples. The envoy of teetotalism was allowed to proceed.

Again, while visiting a Kadi, the Padishah made all preparations for one of his revels ; the Kadi humbly informed him that no drinking had ever been done in his house. Baber countermanded the feast in order not to affront his host.

His love of diversion was not always without danger. One afternoon in autumn, as he was returning to Kabul after one of his excursions, he suggested that they should build a great bonfire of oak-branches, since he was very fond of thier crackling blaze. The sight was stimulating and not unnaturally led to the emptying of innumerable cups with the lords of his suite. Evening came, and he gave the order to break camp. And doubtless they would have gone at once had they been able to sit in their saddles. One of the men of the company was so drunk that he fell to the ground every time he was hoisted on to his horse.

Suddenly a band of Afghan raiders appeared. One of the prince's companions, only slightly sobered by the danger, proposed to cut off his lord's head rather than let him fall into the enemy's hands. He was not easily persuaded to abandon his scheme. The marauders finally were scared off; but it was midnight before the last of the carousers, all swaying like so many stuffed sacks, got safely back to Kabul.

Baber, however, did not permit his pleasures to disorganize his main business of governing. He was not weak. Although he could and did win hearts everywhere by his liberality, his smiling disposition, his gentle poetic spirit and his open and gracious manner, yet when it was necessary his smile vanished and from an iron mouth came merciless commands.

He had no set formula, however. It was by mingling mildness with energy that he gained ascendancy over the Yusufzais, Pathans near Peshawar. He began with a raid and a pyramid of heads; he ended by a marriage with the daughter of their chief, in 1519.

The story is pure Walter Scott:

It appears that one day in the course of an expedition against the Yusufzais, Baber Padishah, disguised as a begging dervish, slipped into the courtyard of the castle of Melik Shah Mansur, head of the clan. It was the holy day of Kurban, and a great gathering was there. From the country round, people had come to offer the traditional compliments of the day to their master. Chiefs and soldiers, doctors of law and clerics, farmers, peasants and shepherds, artisans and merchants, jugglers and musicians—all came to join in the merrymaking.

The daughter of the chief was walking about through the crowd when she caught sight of the rags and patches, the staff and the begging-bowl of one of the Poor of Allah. She ordered a servant to carry the beggar a piece of meat pressed between two slices of bread.

"From whom is this generous gift?" asked the false dervish.

"Bibi Mubaraka, whom Allah hath blessed above all other young women and has given the grace that fills our hearts with pleasure!"

They pointed her out to him. He marvelled at her beauty. And the loquacious servants spread themselves in praises of their young mistress: she was good, she was gay, her spirit was utterly beautiful; and all of her thousand virtues were as yet the property of no man. Moved by this recital, Baber withdrew from the courtyard, climbed a trail into the mountains, and there, seated between two rocks, dreamily ate the sandwich that had come from the charming hand of Bibi Mubaraka.

Then he hurried back to his camp and sent a messenger to Melik with his formal suit for that hand. His proposal was accepted.

The wedding took place. After the feast the Padishah entered the tent of his bride. She stood veiled before him.

"Come! Seat yourself!"

She made a low bow and remained standing.

Twice Baber repeated, "Lift thy veil, O Pathan! And seat thyself!"

She was motionless and silent, until the third time her lord spoke. Then she said, "I have a petition to beg of my lord."

"Speak!"

With her two hands she lifted her skirts: "Imagine, lord, that the people of the Yusufzais lie within the folds of my garment here. Pardon their offences because of me!"

"I do pardon them, unreservedly, and cast them aside with the robe."

Then he led her to the couch, continuing most affably, "I am quite satisfied with you and your tribe," adding with a smile, "and I am satisfied, too, that your uncle Melik Ahmed had something to do with your well-timed plea!"

The affair against the Yusufzais was part of a campaign to reduce all the country lying between the Kunar and the Indus—to-day a portion of the Indian Empire. Baber had commenced it at the end of the year 1518, preferring to fight amid the snows of winter, rather than to brave the spring floods and the intense summer heat.

He was particularly successful in dividing the enemy's house against itself. The Afghan tribe of the Dilazaks had been dispossessed fifty years before by the Yusufzais; he had set the two at each others' throats. The sultans of Bajaur and Swat were vigorous in their opposition to his rule; he permitted the

Yusufzais to invade their territories and so to weaken them.

But his greatest help came from his own army—a small but well disciplined force, efficiently organized and equipped. For the first time he employed the muskets and cannon introduced by the Osmanlis, and engaged the services of a number of specialists in that trade, notably the master-gunner Ali Kuli.

The first city to test the skill of Baber's cannoneer was Bajaur, a strongly fortified town set in the steep mountains that lay between Kunar and the Swat. During the opening minutes of the siege the defenders laughed at the strange roaring bronze tubes. But, when they saw the balls pierce through shield, coat-of-mail and leathern jacket, they stopped laughing.

Eighteen men were shot down on that day. But the fusillade was meant only for intimidation, and was superseded on the morrow by the more ordinary assault of ladders and rams. The walls were scaled and breached. Then, since the population were not Mussulmans, it became a religious duty to massacre the defenders, three thousand of them. The women and children were reserved for slavery. And when the Sultan of Swat heard the news he hastened to surrender without even drawing his sword.

For another three or four months the campaign went on without a single reverse. But war was a business, and Baber was collecting practically no booty. His troops wanted something more than victories. He determined to reward them by a rapid harrying beyond the Indus.

His council advised against the step and pointed

out the many dangers. But their lord's purse was empty and his mind full of ambitious schemes. He was encouraged perhaps by an event in his family at that moment.

One of his wives, Dildar, was near the time of her confinement, and the women of the harem resorted to divination in order to discover the sex of the child. They placed two balls of potter's clay in water, each one containing a slip of paper upon which had been written a name. On one was "Hassan", on the other, "Fatimah". The first to split open displayed "Hassan," to which Baber's mother added "Hindal"—"The Taker of India."

Trusting in the happy omen, Baber set out with a body of light horse about fifteen thousand strong. On the fifteenth of February they crossed the Indus, part by the ford above Attock and part by raft ; on the nineteenth they rode over the Salt Range and stood before Bhera on the banks of the Jhelum, the Hydaspes of Alexander. They had come more than one hundred and twenty miles in four days.

Appalled, the lords of Bhera surrendered at once and paid their ransoms, which amounted to twenty thousand pounds. Khusab, Chenab, and Chiniot followed their example. Baber suddenly was master of all the upper Punjab between the Indus and the Chenab.

Since he considered himself lawful sovereign of the country, in his quality of sole heir of Timur, he treated the inhabitants well, set his governors over them, and strictly forbade his soldiers to rob or harass them. Then, since they were his people, the next logical step was to take them away from the rulers by usurpation, the Afghan kings at Delhi.

Actually, the kings of the moment were as much so by divine right as their Timurid predecessors had been, owing their position equally to force and good fortune—that is to say, to God, the Lord of the Universe. Unfortunately for the divine credit, there is always a great delay in registering the acts of providence, so that a long period elapses before they are recognized as valid.

Timur had robbed the house of Taghlat. The Afghans had ousted Timur's viceroys. Baber did not hesitate. He sent an ambassador to demand the return of his lands. But the man was detained at Lahore by the governor of that city, who forbade him to go any farther. It is difficult to understand Baber's astonishment and indignation at the occurrence.

"These people of Hindustan are incredibly lacking in any sort of judgment and manners, especially the Afghans."

He need not have concerned himself so greatly over his enemies. Scarcely had he gone back to Kabul, on the thirtieth of March, when his friends to whom he had assigned the government of the Punjab abandoned their posts and left the country to its old masters. Delhi was once more very far away, and the Indian summer was hot.

In the interval the expected child was born, and was able to bear the name of Hindal ; and Baber's purpose was further confirmed. The following winter he marched again into his Punjab. He punished the would-be rebels of Bhera, captured the cities of Sialkot and Saidpur, and was riding upon Lahore to make its governor pay for his insolence of the preceding year when he was called home by an invasion of the vexatious Shoujaa Beg, lord of Kandahar.

Baber recognized by this time the absolute necessity of crushing the gadfly and making an end to his city; otherwise his Indian campaigns would be under a continual menace. But it would not be easy business. Kandahar was a fortress of the first magnitude. It was fenced by three encircling walls, heavily bastioned and very high, crowning the summits of three hills that rose sheer out of the plain. Upon the central and loftiest one stood the keep, inaccessible on three sides and approached on the fourth from a precipitous and narrow gorge.

The Padishah laid siege to it in 1520 with all the resources of the period. Famine and plague in his own camp forced him to retire.

He attacked again in 1521. A diplomatic intervention of Shah Ismail brought about another withdrawal.

Finally, in 1522, he made an amicable arrangement with Shoujaa Beg whereby the latter was to abandon the city and go to his spare province, Siwi, that he had cut out for himself in the lower valley of the Indus. Both sides acted with commendable circumspection. When Baber entered Kandahar on the sixth of September, the Arghun soldiers with their wives and goods had been gone two days.

The town, as it rose above the grey plains so high that the clouds seemed part of its bulwarks, appealed to the prince's love of the spectacular. As soon as he was established there he ordered the excavation of the bare flank of the calcareous hill that bore the keep, and built two huge propylaea there, the forty steps of which led to a great gate in the walls guarded by two sculptured panthers. The conception was grandiose ; it was also prophetic.

For now lord Baber was master of all lands between the Amu river, the Indus, Baluchistan and a line running south from Bokhara. His base was ready, a domain won by his courage and diplomacy, a base ready to support something more than a young wanderer's mad dream. Over his wine cups of gold he could gaze towards India and smile.

CHAPTER THIRTEEN

THE STAR OF EMPIRE IN INDIA

THE Indian peninsula lay somewhat outside the normal movement of the sea of Asiatic invasions and conquests which for centuries heaved restlessly between Manchuria and Arabia. Defended on two sides by the ocean, protected on the north by the insurmountable bastions of the Himalayas, it might be approached easily only along the course of the Indus and past Kabul by way of the Khyber Pass.

And even there the aggressors had been repulsed, for as they advanced, suddenly from the plains blew the torrid winds that withered their desires; so that most of them had turned back.

Thickly pcpulated, rich in fruits of the soil and in the treasure collected by old civilizations, it attracted commerce as it invited pillage ; but the dusty swirl and change of its unstable dynasties never appealed to the imaginations of those arch-seekers after empire, the venerable monarchies of China, Persia, and Byzantium.

The very great conquerors—Alexander, the Mongol successors of Genghis Khan, and Timur—appeared for an instant, then vanished. The King of Kings never attempted to leap the barrier of the Indus, and the flood of Arabs was halted before it reached the river. In the sixth century of our era, the mighty Kha Khans, precursors of Genghis, dreamed only of sharing the empire of Darius with the despots of Byzantium. In the eleventh century, the Seljuk Turks spent all their ambition in occupying Iran and the ancient Roman territories.

As a consequence, only the unfortunates of Central Asia ever turned south to India. When a prince was too weak to take from his neighbours, or when he was unable to maintain himself against them in the north, he turned south for compensation, content perforce with the alternative.

One after the other they came, never occupying a very great part of the immense peninsula; they set up their kingdoms one after the other over much the same territories, with the same regularity and precision that the sea encroaches upon certain coastlines.

Already in prehistoric ages the Aryans had spread over the basins of the Indus and the Ganges, crowding their Dravidian predecessors into the south. In the second century before Christ, the descendants of Alexander's soldiers had held ground for a space throughout Transoxiana, Bactria and Khorassan, but were dispossessed by the Yue-chi, nomads from Kan-su on the borders of China. The Greek prince therefore went to the north-west of Hindustan for compensation and, not being able to play the King of Kings save on his coins, made himself a Buddha by imperial decree.

At the same time the Saces, a tribe of Indo-European Scythians, driven out of Seistan by the same Yue-chi, settled at the mouth of the Indus and in Gujarat as the Arghuns of Kandahar had just done in Baber's time. The nomadic Yue-chi in their turn, the following century, were rolled back by the Parthian Arsacids in their movement westward and went into India to replace the Greeks again. But they were not to be in possession long.

In the last years of the fourth century, the Avars of Manchuria drove Attila and his Huns toward Rome,* and the Ephthalite Huns toward Iran. The latter, when Persia broke them and threw them aside, poured into the Punjab, where the climate seemed more favourable.

A little before the year 1000, the Turkish lord of Ghazni threw the net of his power over all Afghanistan and made war successfully upon the Rajah of Lahore, while remaining at grips with the Samanids to the west, until he at last compelled them to cede Khorassan. His son, the great Mahmud (997-1030), within twenty-six years made sixteen triumphal expeditions through India from Kashmir to the mountains of Vindhya, from Gujarat to Oudh. A superlative general, he left no enduring organization save in Punjab. He delighted in plunging the sword of Islam into infidel throats ; he broke the phallic idols of Somnath ; and he carried off heaps of magnificent plunder from Gujarat, which had not been sacked for five centuries.

But his heart remained in Iran. He extended his realm to Ispahan ; and he kept near him as his chief glory the illustrious Firdausi so that the poet might sing in the innumerable couplets of his "Shah Nameh" (at a goldpiece the line) the royal race that had sprung from God whose torch Mahmud hoped to re-kindle.

*"Attila : The Scourge of God," by Marcel Brion.

The Seljuk horsemen soon dissipated his dream. The shepherd clan took and reorganized the Persian empire and sent back to their place the Ghaznavids, who ended without lustre as princes of Lahore.

Upon their ruin arose the Afghan Muhammad, the countryman of Ghor, a ramshackle village fortress. perched in the mountains to the north-west of Kandahar. The extinction of the Seljuks by the Manchus and the Kharesmians (Turks of Khiva) gave him the chance to expand, while the conquests of the Shah of Kharesm, all the lands between the Syr river and Persian Gulf, between Tabriz and Ghazni, pointed the direction—India. For him also it was a *pis-aller*, a gambler's stake. He never settled there; until the day of his murder (1206) he spent his strength in vain efforts to secure a foothold in Iran.

Nevertheless, he penetrated farther into India than any of the conquerors before him, for he reached the southern extremity of Bengal. Instead of contenting himself with the homage of the native princes, he annexed their provinces and put his own viceroy at Delhi. He was the true founder of the Mussulman Empire of India that was to endure until the English came.

His empire was scarcely more than created, before it faced the grave danger of conquest by the irresistible Mongols. These sent invading parties within its borders, but found the country too hot for their liking. Through this aversion alone was it spared, very much as the kingdom of France was saved from the Arabs by its relatively low temperature. It was the snow rather than the Franks that they feared.

It would be an error to label as Afghan that period of Hindustan history which began with the thirteenth century. If Muhammad of Ghor was Afghan, his lieutenant at Delhi was a Turk, as were most of his followers and his successors. He had no male heir, but was always saying, "I have thousands of sons, who will preserve my heritage and repeat prayers for me in the mosque—my Turkish slaves !"

He spoke truly. At his death his viceroy in India, Kutb-ud-Din Aybeg, became the independent sovereign, elected by the Amirs and the generals of the dead monarch. This man was not only a Turk but a slave, bought by the judge of Nishapur and sold by him to Muhammad of Ghor. He was a great and generous giver, a lavish builder, and an able administrator. He espoused the daughter of another Turkish slave elevated to the rank of Vizier, the governor of Ghazni. His own daughter he gave to Altamish, at that time Master of the Hunt and later his successor—also a one-time slave. Of him his contemporary, Minhaj-uz-Siraj, said, "He was unsurpassed for beauty of countenance, for virtue, intelligence and nobility of character."

Thus began one of the most extraordinary royal lines in the history of the world : the Slave Kings of Delhi. Many of them were great. In the fraternity of Islam their servile condition carried with it no stigma. Having developed into efficient servants, they were judged worthy to be masters. The scheme was excellent : it tested ability, gave merit a just reward, and never tolerated mediocrity. It recognized that much depended upon the personal character of a ruler and very little upon his inherited titles. An incompetent son was thrust out if an able bondman could be found. For a hundred years the system justified itself by providing India with genuine rulers.

The thirteenth century belongs to them. Afterward came the dynasties of the Khilji and the Taghlat, both Turkish. Their sovereigns were attached exclusively to India had no ties with the West; and so they sought for one thing alone, the consolidation and extension of the country of their adoption. Their power stretched for the first time beyond the basin of the Ganges to the Deccan. It penetrated to the sources of the Cauvery, including all but the southernmost tip of the peninsula.

Then came Timur, a prince of Iran. He merely passed through, but in such a manner as to be remembered. The incomparable uproar of his gigantic raid, his sackings and his massacres, dazzled the minds of the people after him. Lord of the Terrible, he split the heads of ten thousand prisoners at Batnir and methodically cut the throats of one hundred thousand people of Delhi, by which token his historian recognized him as the true minister of the Wrath of God.

His short campaign in India was a devastating hurricane that destroyed the work of two centuries. Famine and the pest ably seconded the massacres. The cattle were destroyed, the fields abandoned, the social organization was disrupted and the political units were shattered. Those were some of the items on Timur's balance-sheet. The vice-regent placed by him at Multan attempted to maintain an empire at Delhi, and set up a feeble dynasty which soon fell into the hands of the Lodi Afghans. Energetic though they were, these tribesmen could not fit the pieces together again. That miracle was reserved for Baber and his successors.

The mighty land of India, then, was parcelled out among certain great lords, the individual magnificence of whose states was the wonder of Europe.

First was the kingdom of Gujarat. Its shipping had made it an independent power. It counted among its cities the finest ports of Northern India, Cambay, Surat and Broach. The capital, Ahmadabad, contained marvels of architecture. And in it, for more than fifty years, Mahmud Bigarsha reigned.

He was a notable prince; and his was a fabulous appetite. He devoured forty pounds of food a day; and at night he slept between two plates of rice, so that he could awake, eat, and fall back to his sleep without ever being obliged to turn over. "If God had not made me king," he would say, "who could ever have fed me?"

Nevertheless, it was he who prevented the Portuguese from winning a foothold in his states, as they had done in Cochin and Cannanore. He defeated them in a naval battle, with the aid of fifteen Ottoman ships. And it was not until after his death, in 1513, that they succeeded in erecting a trading post at Diu.

Then there was the Central Indian country, Malwa, which had for capital Dhar. A Turkish dynasty came on the heels of the original Afghan rule, and at the time that Baber was delayed at Kabul, was represented by a drunkard who had fifteen thousand women in his harem and who added to the number every pretty girl he saw or heard of. One day while far gone in wine he fell into the lake of his palace garden. He was drowned, and his kingdom was absorbed instantly by Gujarat.

A eunuch created the state of Jaunpur and assumed the title of *King of the Levant*, under which he made his capital renowned for the beauty of its monuments, so that it disputed with Delhi the artistic crown of India.

Bengal, already autonomous before the coming of Timur, was governed by the Hussaynids after 1493. Despite his Arab ancestry, tainted with fanaticism, the founder of the house originated the new cult, *Satyapir*, which pro posed the union of Mussulmans and Hindus. The celebrated Portuguese, Barros, lauds the prosperity of Bengal and the grandeur of its capital at Gaur—a stately city of masonry, nine miles around the walls, with two hundred thousand inhabitants. So crowded were its streets with litters, carts and pedestrians that an attempt at traffic control had been made.

Baber notes as unusual that Nasrat Shah, his contemporary in Bengal, had succeeded his father. Kingship was necessarily of divine appointment; but in the identifying of God's elect, the Bengali had recourse to no common system . . . Every year a great feast was held at Gaur. Whoever during its course succeeded in murdering the king and in actually sitting upon his throne was proclaimed his heir. Thus, before the father of Nasrat Shah a Negro had worn the diadem.

Then there was the Deccan. In 1346 a Turkish

Amir had declared its independence at Deogarh. He rooted his family tree in the Persian King, Bahman, or Ardashir Daradast, whom we call Artaxerxes of the Long Hand. His vast domain rolled westward to the Krishna River and from Goa north to the frontiers of Orissa.

Nikitin, the Russian, who visited it in 1470, has left a picture of its incredible luxury, beside which the "Thousand and one Nights" pales. A noble travelled in a litter of silver, preceded by twenty outriders caparisoned in cloth of gold, and followed by three hundred horsemen, five hundred footmen, ten torchbearers and ten musicians. When the Sultan went to the chase, ten thousand men on horses, fifty thousand men on foot, and two hundred elephants cuirassed in gold accompanied him; and before him marched two hundred trumpeters, one hundred dancers and one hundred concubines. His palace at Gulbarga had seven huge gates, and each one was guarded by a hundred armed men and a hundred scribes who took the names of those who entered and departed. Of one of those Sultans it is related that whenever the number of Hindus massacred at one time reached twenty thousand, it was his custom to indulge in a feast.

In the year of Baber's birth a child of fourteen ascended the throne of the Bahmanids. He lived surrounded by buffoons and mountebanks. "And everybody," says the chronicler, "followed his example; the philosophers pawned their robes in order to go to places of amusement, the teachers quited their classrooms for the tavern." The realm fell to pieces.

A Hindu renegade became ruler at Behar, a Turk at Golconda, a Georgian at Bidar.

In the south, the Hindu rajah of Vijayanagar profited by the confusion to extend his rule over the south of the peninsula, from the Krishna river to Cape Comorin. He became one of the most brilliant sovereigns of his day. And he made his state so invincible that it withstood every Mussulman shock for two centuries. Foreign visitors, such as the Venetian, Niccolo Conti, a certain ambassador of Shah Rukh, and the Portuguese traveller, Paes, vied in picturesque stories about him.

The king was clothed throughout in satin, and wore a collar of pearls so pure and perfect that a jeweller would have been unable to set a price upon the least of them. He possessed twelve thousand wives. Four thousand of them—those assigned to domestic duties——came after him on foot when he travelled; four thousand more followed on horses, and another equal number were carried in litters. Among the latter were two thousand for whom a signal honour was in store: at the death of their husband they would be burned alive.

According to Paes, the army in its full military strength counted seven hundred and three thousand foot-soldiers, thirty-two thousand horsemen, and five hundred and fifty-one elephants, terrible demons as high as mountains and as thundering as the sea. The Rajah took personal command of his forces. He was a robust man of imposing presence, given to physical training, and also to the cultivation of the mind and the spirit.

A man of discernment, he encouraged the study of Sanskrit. A man of universal tastes, he drew to him nobles, priests, courtiers, astrologers, poets and musicians, to heighten the pomp of his jewelled court. His kingdom comprised as many as two hundred provinces ruled by feudal lords, members of the royal family and princes of deposed dynasties.

One might never hear of a city comparable to his capital. It was fortified with seven enclosing walls, of which the outer three embraced fields and gardens, the second three sheltered the bazaars, and the last protected the palace itself. Down the smallest lanes ran streams of fresh water in channels of polished marble. In the market, flowers were sold as objects of necessity, and the jewel merchants offered to their clients in the open, pearls and diamonds, emeralds and rubies. To each magnificently endowed temple was assigned a host of courtesans, whose homes were in the finest streets. These women were rich, honoured above the most noble ladies, and alone of them all were admitted to the presence of the royal wives and tee princesses.

The country boasted three hundred ports, all of them open to foreign commerce. Calicut was chief, and Mangalore (the *Musiris* of the Greeks) still flourished. The Portuguese, whose king wore the title "Lord of Navigation and of the Commerce of Ethiopia, Araby, Persia, and India," owed much of their wealth to the friendliness of the Rajah of Vijayanagar; and they declined in distinction from the day that the Mussulman coalition, in 1565, razed the proud city to the earth.

In the north-west of India, almost lost among the Muhammadan states, was the independent Hindu enclave of Rajputana. Foreign to the soil, the Rajputs had become so native to it as to identify themselves with the military caste of the mythical *Kohatzyas.* They were not a race, but a class of aristocrats isolated in strong castles and organized as an intricate feudal hierarchy of petty chiefs, lords, princes, each at loggerheads with the other owing to rivalries and vendettas.

Such an environment makes fighters. They were notable dogs of war, keen on the scent and always in at the death. Ticklish on a point of honour, vain of the glory of their arms, scornful of the commonalty, and the tradesmen, proud of their chivalrous courtesy, jealous of their privileges and their heroic code, never retreating and never surrendering—Baber found in these men his most stubborn adversaries.

The Lodi Afghans ruled at Delhi over the balance of India—a large state that included the Punjab and stretched to the frontiers of Bengal. When they annexed the province of Jaunpur, they had a kingdom with a circuit of some twelve hundred miles, but they lacked the semblance of government worth the name. They were a kennel of dogs quarrelling over a huge bone.

The country was distributed in fiefs to the lords, and each one regarded himself as his own master by right of his two fists. Sikander, their second Sultan, was vigorous enough to hold them in check; but Ibrahim, who followed him, was less fortunate. Violent and frivolous, brave but vacillating, he was constantly antagonizing his stubborn chiefs and so uniting them against him. Throughout his reign he exhausted himself and his resources in struggling with them.

The man-power of these various states was great enough to have laid the world by the heels, had some force been able to weld it together.

But India was no congeries of rich and poor, of cultivated and unlettered, of soldier and civilian, of princes and subjects. India was both Mussulman and Hindu—more exactly and yet still loosely speaking—and from that circumstance came the lightning that split its strength apart.

To begin with, all the official plums of the government in Hindustan were reserved to the Muhammadans—Turks, and foreigners. They alone could be admitted to the higher ranks in the army. A host of colleges and charitable institutions were devoted to instructing their children and to providing for their poor. Even the Mussulman idler was cared for, since he was regarded as one of the Privileged of Allah.

The Hindus were mere "subjects of the second class." That is to say, they were the "ordinary tax-payers, who gave their gold when the official called for it, and opened their mouths when he wished to spit therein."

One of the Mussulman chroniclers expresses his joy at their distress and degradation, ordered, he says, by a just God. The gratification of the pious, however, can be easily exaggerated; the condition of the Hindu in a Muhammadan state was that of the Christian in the Ottoman Empire—humiliating rather than miserable.

They had no sentiment, pride—in the European

sense—of nationality ; they were indifferent to government, innocent of political ambition and hence incapable of forming a stable unit. They were deaf to all problems save one, religion. But when that was raised they became alert, and their blood clamoured for the massacre of the infidel Muhammadan.

The latter, of course, discovered *their* infidels in the Hindus. A Muhammadan sovereign drew all his power from God. In return for the divine sufferance he must execute God's laws, exterminate idolatry, and smother heresy. But the Turks were by nature less fanatical than the Hindus and still are. Compare the native India and native Turkey of to-day.

The great Ala-ud-Din, two hundred years before Baber's time, declared himself the vicar of God in all things temporal. The clergy were barred from interference. He once said to an illustrious doctor, "I do what I believe to be good for the state and suited to the time ; as a ruler I am very little concerned over the Last Judgment."

But, in general, creed entered into and guided the policies of government, and served to bring all Mussulmans together in a common cause against the unbeliever. The Turks were almost compelled to be as jealous of their dogmas as were the Hindus. The Arab writer, Albiruni, very justly said, "Our religion makes impossible any understanding with infidels, and digs an abyss between ourselves and them." And thus the country was effectively prevented from uniting against a common foe, against invasion.

The more active minds among the Hindus realized the danger and the absurdity of the situation. They sought to remedy the pernicious condition by a subtle reconciliation of Brahmanic and Islamic doctrines. They pronounced against the excess of formal ceremony and against the caste system ; and they affirmed the equality of Hindu and Muhammadan before God.

"Purity of heart," said Kabir, the weaver of Benares, "is of more importance than a bath in the Ganges. Hindu and Turk are of the same clay. And all who do good are brothers."

The triumph of such a conception would have altered the course of India's history ; against the bulwarks of tradition it was impotent. The ideas of philosophers create a revolution only when they strike a responsive chord in the hearts of the masses.

Such was the Indian scene when Baber cast the die of his resolution.

He did not do it lightly. The Padishah was too wise a man to draw his hope of a new empire from the two words "disorder" and "anarchy." India might be in political chaos; but Vijayanagar could put a million men in the field. India might be the nesting-place of anarchy ; but ten thousand Rajputs had once slaughtered forty thousand Mongols. Baber knew the kings of the peninsula for what they were—brave and powerful lords.

But he also knew of almost invincible allies against them—the superior stamina and military skill of his northern men.

The Panther of Farghana, whom his enemies would call the Tiger, settled back upon his haunches, his muscles gathered for the fateful leap.

CHAPTER FOURTEEN

THE KILL OF THE TIGER

THE handsome and truculent Ibrahim Lodi multiplied his rigours at Delhi. Mian Bhua, the illustrious vizier of his father, was first thrown into prison and then given a cup of poisoned wine. Azam Humayun, lord of the Sarwanis, and conqueror of the Rajputs, was assassinated in his dungeon. Hussayn Khan Farmuli had his throat cut while asleep. The country was in an uproar. Several of his greatest vassals revolted and set up an independent state at Bihar.

Daulat Khan Lodi, the governor of Lahore, was ordered to appear at Delhi ; he excused himself. His son, Dilawar Khan, whom he sent in his place, was conducted to prison and there shown the bodies of rebels hanging from the walls.

"Now you know," remarked the Sultan, "what awaits those who venture to disobey me !" Then his army marched against Daulat Khan.

The latter appealed to Baber. His son presented himself at Kabul in behalf of his father and spoke of the fury among the nobles and of the discontent in the army. He considered it time to intervene.

"For thirty years," Baber said to him, "you have eaten the salt of Lord Ibrahim and of his father. Why do you abandon him so abruptly ?"

"It is true that my father and grandfather spent forty perilous years in his service. But the man persecutes the most faithful of his vassals. Without cause he has put to death twenty-three of his best men and has ruined their families. Some he has spitted upon hooks, and they dangle now from the battlements; others he has burned alive. That is why the nobles have sent me to you to convey their homage. They await you anxiously."

"Then," reports Ahmed Yadgar the historian, "Baber passed the entire night in walking about his garden. When dawn brightened in the sky he lifted up the hands of prayer: 'O God! If India will belong to me, give me a sign! Let the fruits of that country, the betel-leaf and the mango, be brought before me to-day. I shall accept them as a favourable omen.'"

And at the morning audience Dilawar, presenting himself again, offered the Padishah the ritual gifts that he had brought from his father. Among them were betel-leaves and half ripe mangoes preserved in honey.

At sight of them Baber recognized the hand of God beckoning him south to the throne of an empire. And to Dilawar, His instrument, he gave lavish presents—for him a blooded horse and a robe of honour, for his father ten racing horses of Irak and many fine pieces of fabric.

The prelude of his great campaign remains obscure to this day. Here again the Memoirs are lacking; they contain no record of events from the second of January, 1520, to the sixteenth of November, 1525, six years that are of especial interest since they were occupied with the preparations already discussed and several more foraying expeditions into India, some against recalcitrant Kandahar, Badakshan and Balkh, and others against rebel tribes. Besides, during this period he found time to compose for a son his didactic poem, two thousand lines long, on the Mussulman religion.

The lost pages could not but clarify the Indian intrigues that hedged Baber's path of conquest. As it is, we know only that Daulat Khan had leagued with Alim Khan, an uncle of Ibrahim's to place him on the throne of his nephew, and that the claimant himself came to Kabul to enlist the aid of the Padishah.

The usual delays cropped up. Late in the autumn of 1523 Baber set out, met and vanquished the army that Ibrahim had dispatched against Daulat Khan, and then went on to Dipalpur. Here the Khan, dissatisfied with the minor role that Baber had left him to play, deserted with his forces and disappeared into the foothills of the Himalayas.

Baber was compelled to fall back. The Punjab was threatened by the two traitors Daulat and Alim Khan; Shah Ismail's death in Persia had set loose rebellion among the Uzbeks; Baber's presence was imperative in the north-west.

Fortunately, his Turkish governors in the Punjab were faithful. Having settled with the Uzbek wolves, Baber was once more ready to return to his Indian muttons and to make short shrift of the two jackal Khans who had been sniffing around moribund Delhi.

Henceforward the Padishah resolved to have done with trading, and bartering, and timorous measures, and reliance upon others. He determined to risk everything. At first he had spoken diplomatically with the Lodi Afghans; now he refers to "the countries which from time immemorial have been ours." Now he treats the great Afghan lords as vessals. It is no longer one of Timur's descendants who speaks, but the commander of the Turks, Zahir-ud-Din Muhammad—Baber—The Tiger. And in obedience to his imperious will Destiny unveils an immense prospect.

On Friday the seventeenth of November, 1525, the man departed on his fifth and last expedition into his future empire, without a trace of that pomposity with which another might have felt obliged to adorn the occasion. He set out as simply and gaily as if bound on a holiday.

For eight days he lingered with his army near his delicious Gardens of Fidelity on the banks of the Kabul, waiting for the ever-tardy Humayun. And there he tasted the pleasures of home for the last time.

There were joyous evenings, and after them joyous mornings, where hashish prolonged the dreams drained from his wine cups. He floated down the stream on his barge, feasting with the men of his suite. Or late at night, cup in hand, he stood upon a hill that overlooked the east, watching for the dawn to outflame the myriad campfires of his army. With morning he mounted his horse and hunted the rhinoceros and so skilfully that the ferocious beast never charged the huntsmen but fled before the elephants. He read and composed poetry with his lettered companions; and one day, having hit upon a couplet form that delighted him, he bade the whole company compose obscene drinking-songs upon that model. But an immediate seizure of violent cramp persuaded him that he had sinned against his mother-tongue; he resolved to give up such frivolous practices.

Humayun arrived at last and was severely reprimanded for his delay. Then the army marched quickly to the barrier of the Indus. They found boats waiting. The business of embarkation was put into the hands of six or seven competent officers, who, assisted by a large staff of secretaries, set down the name of every soldier as he entered his boat. "Good and bad," they totalled twelve thousand.*

The passage of the Indus took place on the fifteenth of December. Marching at the leisurely rate of fifteen miles a day Baber took his course to the north of Lahore over the foothills of the mountains and in the direction of Sialkot. For there only could he find the grain needed to provision his troops, the plains having withered under an unusually dry season.

He knew, however, that he could not undertake a southern campaign with the traitorous Daulat Khan hovering in his rear. The man had to be eliminated. With this in mind Baber halted and sent orders to all the lords he had left in the Punjab to rejoin him. Then, when he had learned from his scouts of the position of the enemy, he advanced in force.

The Khan's troops lay on the banks of the Ravi, near Lahore. When they got wind of his approach

* See Appendix C.

they fled without waiting for him. Old Daulat Khan himself hid in his mountain castle at Milwat, some hundred miles from Lahore ; but he was dragged out of it and down to his ally, to tender his submission in person. He did so, but with a very ill grace, brimming with excuses. When he hesitated to kneel, Baber had him hauled to the presence by the heels.

Harsh words followed: "I treated you generously, as though you had been my father. I gave you a dependency worth a kingdom, and you return my favours by denying me your help, by invading my territories and fomenting trouble and discord there like a traitor!"

"The stupid old fool knew not what to answer!" said Baber—who did not love those who resisted him. Nevertheless, generous as was ever his habit, he set at liberty the wives and family of Daulat Khan, and personally superintended their departure from the castle. After they had gone, he entered.

Ghasi Khan, the wealthiest member of the Daulet clan, unable to shoot the moon, had left his household and goods to the tender mercies of the enemy. Baber first appraised the beautiful library collected by "that book-armed coward," then leaped astride his horse and was off in pursuit of the amateur of rare volumes, harrying him through the steep gorges of the mountains but never quite catching him.

Leaving the chase, therefore, to a flying column, he turned back to risk the supreme adventure.

Once again upon a new terrain, he advances slowly and carefully. No organized opposition against him as yet! But he must fix his authority in each district as he passes through it; wipe out anything but subservient mountaineers in the mountains on his left flank. Along the way he receives the submission of a number of Afghan nobles, one of whom presumes to sit down in his presence. "These Afghans are barren of all tact."

He crosses the Sutlej at Ropur and reaches Ambala. While exploring the environs one day, he comes upon a charming valley through which tumbles a little stream. There he plants an avenue of trees. He arrives at the Jumna; his curiosity leads him to the tomb of a saint venerated alike by Hindu and Mussulman. And as he walks he takes hashish in order to highten his pleasure. Beneath a cluster of living green gushes a spring.

"Sire," remarks Tardi Beg Khaksar, "here is a pleasant spot for so villainous a country."

"It is yours," answer the prince.

At last the Sultan of Delhi, who had allowed Baber to march unimpeded through his country four hundred miles beyond the Indus, came out to fight. He had consulted his astrologers and had been given a neatly ambiguous forecast. Understanding that he was to be victorious, he entered upon his campaign full of high hope. That of his astrologers was less rosy; in fact, they seemed to pin very little faith in the stars, for they deserted their master—and wisely, too, as the event proved.

While the bulk of Ibrahim's forces marched due north from Delhi along the right bank of the Jumna, a secondary force moved up from Hissar-Firuza in the south-west, and bore down upon Baber's right wing, commanded by Humayun, then eighteen years of age. The lad scattered the Indians easily and brought his father a hundred prisoners, with seven or eight elephants as trophies of the victory. In recompense, his father made him lord of Hissar-Firuza and its revenues.

For another two days Baber followed the course of the river towards Delhi. Then, having secret information from his scouts, he suddenly threw out a detachment to his left : a flanking movement of the enemy was uncovered, the Sultan's division was routed and driven back to the south, and Baber added seventy prisoners and six elephants to his train.

It was now the first of April, 1526. Baber had reached Panipat, in the plain where so many times before the fate of India had beed decided. It was a dreary, barren waste, rolling out through silence over yellow flats, dry and naked, broken here and there only by thorny bush. Across it Ibrahim approached ; and Baber deployed his army "... less numerous," he says, "than I had thought." For, while he had recruited men as he advanced, he had also garrisoned the towns from his small force.

Prudently, he took up a defensive position. He based his right flank solidly upon the outlying gardens of the town. A ditch and an extensive *abattis* protected his left. His front lay behind a line of seven hundred carts tied together with heavy strips of raw-hide to break cavalry charges. In the space between each pair were *turas*, mantelets or moveable parapets, in the shelter of which the matchlocks might be fired with security. Passages had been provided—an arrow's flight apart—wide enough to permit a hundred and fifty horsemen to ride abreast through them.

One of the chiefs observed that the enemy would not attack such perfect defences. "My friend," answered Baber, "we must not judge these people as though they were Uzbeks, who know how to fight. When I evacuated Samarkand and barricaded myself in the streets of Hissar, those who were my enemies then were too experienced to storm my defences. But these to-day are incapable of conceiving or executing any sensible manoeuvre. They cannot even march and halt intelligently."

"In fact," he confides to his Memoirs, "God disposed everything for the best, and the battle ended as I had foreseen."

For eight days he awaited Ibrahim's attack. The soldiers were restless. They felt like prisoners, so far away from their homes and in the midst of strange men and strange things. They were even frightened ; for the rumour was abroad that Ibrahim had one hundred thousand men under him, and one hundred warelephants.

But he, according to Baber, was as clumsy as he was miserly. He marched erratically and without plan ; and he could not bring himself to spent any part of his treasure on a few thousand fresh recruits, as he might well have done. The size of his army is not known precisely. "The Chronicle of the Afghan Sultans" *puts it at fifty thousand soldiers. It is certain* only that he greatly outnumbered Baber's small body.

In spite of that, he was timorous and would not

strike. The Padishah tired of waiting. On the night of the ninth day he delivered a surprise attack with four or five thousand men. It was a feint and one that succeeded, for the enemy was drawn into assuming the offensive.

Ibrahim was elated at the ease with which the invaders had been repulsed. And at dawn on the twenty-first of April, 1526, he moved up in order of battle. Instantly warned of the movement, the leader of the Mongols bade his men put on their helmets, and then disposed them according to the traditional formation of the Turks and Mongols : centre, right wing, left wing, vanguard, reserve, and, outside each wing, a flying column stationed there to execute the time-honoured flanking movement.

The army of Delhi advanced rapidly. When they were near enough to observe the terrifying, disciplined ranks of the Turks and the bristling of all that unfamiliar defensive work, their attack lost its momentum. But those behind still pressed forward, and the lines were thrown into confusion.

Baber seized the moment and sent out his flanking columns to envelop the army of the Indians, while the two wings charged straight on. In the centre Ali Kuli with his great cannon, and Mustafa with his mobile culverins roused terror as well as playing havoc.

But, as usual, the horsemen and archers were the mainstay of Baber's offence. One of the reasons for the superiority of the Turco-Mongolian bow as an instrument of war lay in the fact that it was the arm of the nobles—that is to say, of the finest warriors—and not, as in continental Europe of spiritless rustics.

The English archers owned their prowess partly to their station as yeomen, relatively independent and respected ; but fighting was not their profession. Furthermore, the ordinary bow in the hands of a Turk would shoot three times as rapidly as a musket, even in Bernier's time ; and it could kill at two hundred yards.

The enemy's centre gave way under the counter-attack ; and his troops, beset on all sides and jammed into a narrow space, fluoundered about in desperate confusion. The battle had been engaged at nine o'clock, "when the sun stood a javelin's height above the horizon" ; it was over at midday. The great mob from Delhi was utterly defeated, and when they fled, they left twenty thousand dead and wounded on the field.

In a place where the fighting had been fiercest, dead amid a heap of the slain of his sword lay the vain and foolish, but courageous, Ibrahim. His head was struck off and carried to Baber.

There is a variant to this episode in "The Chronicle of the Afghan Sultans." It claims that the victorious prince, as he walked over the field after the battle, discovered the dead Sultan in the midst of those whom he had killed. He approached, lifted up the head of his foe, and said, "Let there be honour paid to his valour !"—and ordered the body to be washed, and then buried on the spot where the Sultan had met his death... This tale has more of rhetoric than truth about it.

While he energetically pursued the routed army, Baber sent couriers to Delhi and Agra to take over the citadels and put his seal upon the treasuries. He made his entry into the former city on the twenty-fourth of the month. Piously he visited the mausoleums and monuments of the great Sultans of the past, the symbols of Turkish glory and wonders of art.

On Friday the twenty-seventh public prayers were said in his name by the Sheik. God had set the seal of His approval upon Zahir-ud-Din Muhammad, surnamed the Panther, Emperor of India and First of the Moguls.

Two weeks later the new sovereign entered Agra, where his son presented him, by way of homage, with the famous Kohi-nur diamond, which had been given him by the sons of the dead Rajah of Gwalior whom he had chivalrously guarded during the sack of the town. The worth of the stone, according to Baber, was sufficient to have clothed and fed the entire world for twenty-four hours. One hundred and forty years later, the celebrated traveller and collector of gems, Tavernier, estimated its weight at two hundred and seventy-nine carats* and its value at eleven million, seven hundred and twenty-three thousand two hundred and seventy-eight *livres*.

Baber returned it to his son.

Next came the brave day of the distribution of booty. A sum the equivalent of six hundred thousand pounds—not reckoning the far higher purchasing power—went to Humayun, who had played his part like a man in the great battle. Four hundred thousand went to each of the chief Begs. A prize in silver was

*The Koh-i-nur was said to have weighed at the very least 790 carats when found. It weighed a little more than 186 carats when given to Queen Victoria in 1850. By recutting it was further reduced to 106 carats.

given to every soldier in the army according to his rank ; even the servants and grooms were not neglected. The poets, the scribes and the traders who had accompanied the expedition received their share.

Baber sent to his children and to the members of his family at Kabul millions in gold, unbored pearls and ingots of silver, gems without price, and retinues of slaves. The old friends and the pious Sheiks of Samarkand, Khorassan, and Irak, and the guardians of the sanctuaries at Mecca and Medina drank at the flood of his munificence. To every inhabitant of the principality of Kabul, male and female, adult and child, free and slave, went the gift of a piece of silver, in order that they might all rejoice in their master's triumph. The imperial liberality did not overlook Baber himself, the one-time Calender, the wandering mendicant of Allah.

But after that came the real difficulties.

The underlings of the dead king, Afghans for the most part, rose against the upstart emperor. Those in the west, in Sambhal, Dholpur, and even in towns near Agra, found a pretender in the person of Ibrahim's brother. In the east the Sultan of the insurgents was killed; but his place was taken at once by his son. The native population supported their own chieftains in resisting the usurper. The village folk, having no more livestock or grain, took to the highways and turned robbers, so that travel became dangerous.

"It is a land barren of all delight," said Baber ; "depressingly uniform, flat, without any running streams other than the sluggish rivers ; and nothing grows but miserable clumps of thorn-trees that serve as hiding-places for the rebels."

In one respect, indeed, he had been most unlucky: his conquest had been achieved at the most trying season and in a year that proved unrelentingly hot. The trees and plants were scorched ; even their roots dried up. The sun split the arid soil and drew from it a killing shroud of haze and dust. The simoon blew, and the unhappy warriors could neither eat nor sleep. Clamorously they demanded to be taken away from this hell.

Especially did the new lords created by the emperor not care to earn his favours by patience in the face of slow death. The older ones as well were sullen ; they grumbled —why must the pirates remain on the accursed ship after they had looted it ? None showed more disgust than Khoja Kelan. Ancient, energetic, devoted, he had served Baber indefatigably, he had played with the child, watched over the youth, and fought without rest at the side of the grown man, a guide to follow in the council as well as in the saddle, a fighter whose six brothers had perished in harness. Yet the heat of India was burning away these ties.

This attitude on the part of the most faithful was especially discouraging to Baber because "I had never undertaken any project without the full consent of my companions." Undoubtedly it must have required several years to persuade his chiefs to follow him into India, so much did they distrust a strange country. But finally they had consented, they had approved.

In desperation he called a meeting of the lords and

pointed out that it was impossible to be a king without territories and subjects ; that here they had acquired the necessary lands and people ; that Kabul, Kandahar and Kunduz were unfruitful countries, incapable of sustaining men such as they ; that it was unreasonable to renounce the fruits of their heroic courage, of their hardships and of the dangers they had surmounted merely to return at last to the poverty they had left.

The majority of them gave in. But Khoja Kelan would listen to nothing. He asked for and obtained his dismissal – and also the governorship of Ghazni, together with a post of confidence near the royal family in Kabul. When he left for home he was charged with the delivery of gifts to the ladies of the harem, notably with a bevy of dancers belonging to the dead Rajah, one to each lady.

As he departed, he scratched upon a wall of the palace this epigram of his own composition :

The Indus crossed, may my face turn black,
If ever I feel the wish to turn back.

Baber saw the lines, and had the last word. Beneath them he scratched these Persian verses :

Give thanks, O Baber, to God, the Good, the Generous
Who has given you India and its broad kingdoms !
If ever the fires of its sky weary you, if the cold
Of the North leaves one regret in your heart,
Go to——Ghazni !

A proverb ran, "God did not need to invent hell He already had Ghazni."

In his Memoirs, on the other hand, the emperor gives this candid opinion of his empire. "The country has little to recommend it. The inhabitants are not handsome, they have no idea of the pleasure of society, no genius or talent, neither polish of manner, amiability nor sympathetic feeling, neither ingenuity nor mechanical inventiveness, nor knowledge or skill in architecture. They have no decent houses, good fruits, ice, or cold water ; their markets are ill-supplied ; they have neither public baths nor colleges ; neither candles nor candlesticks. If you want to read or write by night, you must have a filthy half-naked fellow standing over you with a flaring torch."

He therefore set about introducing a few of the graces of living into the land of his adoption, also began to fight against its three principal drawbacks : the heat, the dust, and the wind.

He made incessant search around Agra for a position for his gardens. He found only such unpromising terrain that once he was on the point of abandoning his project. But he was determined not to live in a place less beautiful than Kabul. He dug a great well, installed water-wheels, built reservoirs and fountains, laid out and planted gardens and parterres near them, "full of grace and symmetry, wherein roses and narcissi were set with perfect art"

Many of the lords followed his example. They also played with their pleached walks, their running streams and their pools, whose delicious coolness could make them forget the heat of the wind beyond their gardens.

Seeing that Baber evidently meant to stay, the

Afghan nobles laid down their arms. Sheik Kuron of Koil, a musician second to none, presented his lord with two thousand archers. Ali Khan Farmuli surrendered, at the modest price of twenty thousand pounds. And—a greater consequence—the heads of the army sent by Ibrahim against the rebels in the west offered their services to Baber in the taking of new provinces. Baber accepted, they were paid for their generosity, each one receiving a sum that varied from sixteen thousand to one hundred thousand pounds.

There remained, none the less, certain headstrong chiefs who did not abandon hostilities. Most important among them was Rana Sanga, king of the Rajputs in the west. Another raised the standard of insurrection in the east, along the upper reaches of the Ganges. The council determined to obliterate the latter at once.

The monarch remained at Agra in order to keep in touch with all his various schemes, sending Humayun to command the army in the field. The young lad did well. He crossed the Ganges, pushed the enemy back beyond the Gogra, captured Jaunpur and Ghazipur, and then returned in November at the command of his father in order to arrest the advance of Rana Sanga.

Meanwhile, the emperor, more by diplomacy and money than by force, laid his hand upon the neighbouring fortified towns that were still independent. Their names were Etah, Bhiwani, Dholpur and Gwalior. He did not consider them of great importance ; yet the combined man-power of their states was well over five million.

So that when the year 1526 approached its term he was master of northern India, to the borders of Behar, an eagle's flight of a long thousand miles from his citadel in Kabul. He was no longer Padishah in name only.

CHAPTER FIFTEEN

BABER PROVES HIMSELF EMPEROR

RANA SANHRAM SINGH, king of the fiery Rajput chivalry, was a worthy foe. More commonly known as Rana Sanga, he had begun as an inconspicuous Rajah at Udaipur, but had risen through his genius of command to be the revered head of all the Hindu lords.

He was incontestably supreme. In the course of innumerable combats against the enemies of his race, sustained with as much tenacity as brilliance, the battered old hero had lost an arm and an eye, and he carried a broken leg and twenty-four scars. It was reported that he could place himself at the head of seven Rajahs, one hundred and four chieftains, eighty thousand horsemen and five hundren elephants. When his drums beat, war followed !

At the beginning he had shown friendship toward Baber, Lord of Afghanistan ; he had sent ambassadors to him at Kabul and had even joined with him against Ibrahim. But his attitude changed when Baber threatened to become a fixture. He disappointed his ally. For a time he remained neutral, then he disputed with the emperor the towns along the frontier. And now he was in open war against him.

It was with good reason, then, that Humayun's army hurried back to Agra on the sixth of January.

Heretofore the emperor had fought against fellow-Mussulmans. Now he set himself against the Hindus : it was to be a *jihad*,, a Holy War !

And on the eleventh of the next month he marched against the infidels. He looked for a swift decision. His master-gunner, Ali Kuli, had just cast a great bronze cannon specially for the campaign, whose ball would carry sixteen hundred paces. In recompense he had received a rich dagger, a robe of honour, and a thoroughbred horse. The emperor hoped for quick results from his gunner's monster.

The campaign opened unfortunately. A first skirmish was a defeat Revolt flared up everywhere. Raberi, Chandwar and Sambhal fell into the enemy's hands. Gwalior was bottled up, Kanauj was abandoned. The Hindu chiefs who had joined the emperor deserted. His army was restless; there were murmured demands to retire to the safe Punjab. A famous astrologer spread alarming predictions. So Baber himself, believing only in favourable signs, gave the "lying rascal" to understand, as he drove him out of the country, the astrology was admirable only when it was optimistic.

Something had to be done to raise the morale of his soldiers. He therefore issued a proclamation appealing to their sentiments of honour and religion. He quoted from the poet Firdausi :

Let me die honourably and I die content ,
To the earth my body, but to the heavens my honour.

Everyone was made to swear upon the Koran not

to leave the fight against the infidels until his soul had departed his body.

He bolstered up this abstract appeal by remitting certain stamp duties. Then, considering that insufficient, he solemnly broke his wine cups before the eyes of the entire army, and bade them renounce the evil habit of drinking.

For his part, he not only took the vow but kept it, though the keeping was hard. Writing the next year to his old friend Khoja Kelan on the subject, he says, "The others repented of their oath and are now doing penance. For myself, the observance of it is punishment enough."

But the pledge served to give his men a good opinion of themselves. Their morale improved immediately.

And Now Baber was ready for the enemy. He made sure of every detail of defence; he threw up earthworks and placed his line of carts and movable parapets in front of them. Then he went forward a mile to a position similarly prepared, near Kanwaha.

The thoroughness of his preparations is revealed by his Memoirs: "I advanced my wagons with all the apparatus and war-engines that I had prepared, and marched forward with my army in order of battle—right wing, left wing and centre in their places. In front were the wagons and gun-carriages, and in their rear came Ali Kuli with a body of his matchlock men to prevent communication from being cut off between the artillery and the infantry behind them, and to enable them to advance and to form in line.

"When the ranks were drawn up and every man in his place, I galloped along the line, encouraging the

Begs and the men of the centre, right and left, giving special directions to each division how to act and to each man orders how to proceed and engage. Then, when that was done, I moved the army on in battle array."

The tactics to be employed were those of the battle of Panipat: a frontal attack delivered by the wings, an enveloping movement by the flanking columns, cannonade and fusillade from the centre, reinforcements hurried to every weak point either by troops of the line or by the strong reserve held to the rear, then the powerful centre hurled forward at the last moment.

The meeting finally took place on the twelfth of March, New Year's day of his calendar. The fight began with a magnificent charge of the Rajputani upon the Turkish right. Baber immediately threw in reserves to support that point, and ordered his artillery to open fire.

There was no stopping the charge of the superb Rajputani, however. On they came, division after division, wave after wave, up to the very mouths of the cannon. The struggle was desperate.

But the Hindus suffered from a fatal lack of co-operation and precision in their manoeuvres. After several hours of close and doubtful fighting, Baber gave orders to couriers who galloped off to where the flanking columns sat their horses, motionless and silent apart from the conflict—fresh shock troops all primed to take the heart out of the battle-weary foe.

Their commanders shouted, wheeled, and drew

their swords. The lightning flash of steel was followed by the thunder of horsemen executing the famous turning movement of the Mongols.

At the same time the emperor ordered his guns forward and sent out the household troops at the gallop on either side of his centre of fusiliers who advanced firing.

Indians cannot fight when taken in the rear. The Rajputs were rolled back in confusion, and the battle became a massacre. Ali Kuli's "huge balls" tore great holes in their ranks. The furious rain of arrows from the powerful unerring bows of the Mongols and Turks covered the ground with dead. So at least India's most splendid chivalry broke and fled, leaving behind them the flower of their order, "who exchanged this dwelling of clay for the pits of hell." And the noblest heads of Rajputana were heaped in a ghastly pyramid by the conqueror.

Hassan Khan, the chief Afghan rebel, died of a musket ball wound. Rana Sanga escaped, thinking to take refuge with the Sultan of Gujarat. And Baber assumed the title of Ghazi—Victor for the Faith.

The council that was held immediately after the victory decided that an invasion of the Rajput territories would be unwise at the moment because of the heat and the scarcity of water along the route. The victors therefore limited their activities to the subjection of the province of Mewat and the recapture of the cities that had been lost.

The onset of the rainy season would soon put an end to the campaign. So the Padishah proceeded to a general distribution of fiefs. When that was done, he allowed each vassal to retire to his post and gave leaves of absence to those who wished to go back to Central Asia. He relieved from further duty the contingents from Badakshan, who were unaccustomed to serving for more than a month or two at a time, and ordered Humayun to accompany them and resume charge of that province.

That young man, with honours and riches heaped upon him, revealed his true character. As he passed through Delhi he delayed long enough to break open the public treasury and plunder it. For which Baber punished this favourite son of his, the only child of his cherished Maham, by writing him a letter of reprimand.

The rains came, but Baber was not inactive. He made an extended tour through the country near his capital. Three times he visited Sikri and celebrated there, in his Garden of Victory, the Feast of the Breaking of Fast. At Dholpur he found a huge boulder of such superb red that he ordered a house to be carved out of it. He visited Bari, Koil and Sambhal. He took boat and sailed down the river to Delhi again, to meet his paternal aunts, who had come to see him. While entertaining them he fell ill of grippe and quinsy. Then he undertook a pious course of reading, and repeated it forty-one times. In addition, he wrote a treatise upon poetry, wherein he demonstrated the five hundred and four different kinds of caesura.

His illness left him with the rains. On the ninth of December he recommenced his Holy War by an expedition against Chanderi, on the eastern edge of Rajputana. By horse and boat he followed the course of the Jumna to Kalpi. From that point he marched straight to his goal, cutting and levelling his own road through the jungle, holding his course for six weeks through the miasmal mist of the swamps and the haunts of savage beasts, leaving behind him hundreds of men and horses dead of fever and snake-bite, yet firm in his resolve topunish the rebels.

On the twentieth of January, 1528, he burst out of the streaming shadows of the forest into a clearing before the rebel city, perched upon a pinnacle of rock within an arm of the sluggish Batwa River. And when he had deployed his troops over the yielding moss and the tufts of marsh weed, the siege of one of India's greatest strongholds was begun.

The walls of the town rose more than two hundred feet above the level of the yellow stream, and were secured on the north side by a treacherous swamp, and guarded on the west and south by the river. Only by the steep rocky slope eastward was the town accessible: and on that side two bastions jutted out of ramparts twenty feet high.

As if impaled on the very point of the needle, two hundred and thirty feet above the town itself, hung the central keep with a vast cistern hollowed out of the rock, seemingly immune from assault and starvation.

The emperor, now a seasoned campaigner with an eye to his man-power, invited a compromise. To Medini Rao, the governor, he sent word suggesting that he should listen to a proposal of exchange. Would this brave worthy give up Chanderi for some rich city on the Ganges? He would not. So preparations were made for an assault.

For a week the army constructed screens and ladders, cut timbers and bolted them into the frames, arms, and counterweights of catapults and mangonels. The stalwart Ali Kuli mounted and sighted his light pieces—the only ones he could bring over the jungle road. And, under cover of night, the engineers sank two deep mines into the base of the cliff-like eastern ramparts, wedging stout beams against the roofs of their tunnels as they drove deeper.

On the morning of the eighth day Baber gave the signal for the attack. The oil-soaked timbers within the mines were fired. And suddenly with a crash and roar, half the face of the eastern wall crumbled and fell outward in a great smoking mass, exposing houses and streets within the town. Then the war drums sounded the advance, and the Turks scrambled over the debris to the attack, covered by a furious discharge of arrows from two of their divisions stationed to right and left of the breach.

The Hindus could not face the deadly rain. They fell back from the ruinous rift and were beaten back into the citadel, leaving their town in the hands of the emperor by nightfall. And he, knowing that his men were exhausted by the hard fighting and sleepless nights on the river-marshes, silenced the drums and recalled his soldiers.

The next morning they attempted to carry the keep. But at its foot, for a long time, they won nothing but death. Rocks were hurled down at them, and coming from that great height, crushed them through their very screens. The scaling ladders were too short; and when by joining several together, they succeeded in raising two of them, one was flung backward to eternity, while the other, planted more securely, was swept clean by a bucket of boiling pitch. The assailants on the ledges below steamed under a merciless sun. Their Turkish arrows, usually winged with death, were ineffectual at such an angle, and either fell harmlessly within the courtyard of the citadel or overshot it. As for the missiles from culcerin and mangonel, these glancing from the battlements, proved boomerangs deadly to their senders.

The Hindus laughed from their eagle's nest. Medini Rao stood within an embrasure and spat in the direction of Baber's standard.

The latter had as yet found no answer to the problem set him ; and the heap of the Turkish dead grew apace, filling the air with the stench of blood so that a guard had to be posted on the jungle edge to drive off the man-eaters.

It was then that Baber's lucky star seemed in the ascendant again. A man was brought before him with a suggestive story. He had gone through a house close to the north wall and there had discovered a hidden way which he had followed up an incline until, in the dark, he had been assailed by an unknown number of the enemy from whom he had barely escaped with his life.

By a happy coincidence at this same instant, high over their heads came a triumphant shout in Turkish. Looking up, they beheld the gates of the fortress swing open and reveal a certain Shaham Nur Beg, a warrior of little note until this moment which found him holding the enemy at bay single-handed.

He had found a bastion of the town wall that connected with the ramparts of the keep and had dared climb it. Dropping without warning into the *enceinte*, he had cut his way through a number of the surprised garrison, had won to the gate-tower, and before he could be checked had thrown wide the gates.

His comrades gave an answering shout and rushed up the narrow path to his rescue. At once Baber ordered his bodyguard into the hidden shaft, and with his reserve gave Shaham Nur Beg his own immediate support.

Resistance was soon at an end. When the desperate garrison saw the Turks spring up among them, some, true to their heroic code, threw themselves naked upon the Muhammadan swords, the others slew their women, then gathered in a circle and hacked simultaneously at one another's necks. After that, the Rajputs of Chanderi troubled Baber no more. The insult to his standard was avenged by another pyramid of heads.

During the siege a messenger had come to Baber from his army in the east. Imperturbably the emperor had listened to the man, then without a word had gone under the very walls of the fortress to hearten his soldiers. But the news which he had received was a severe blow. Lucknow and Kanauj, the prizes of the battle of Kanwaha, were lost to him again.

Now, therefore, he renounced his plan for the further subjugation of Rajputana and marched straight upon the presumptuous insurgents, who held the towns under the command of the Afghan, Biban Jilwani, a man who had once presumed to seat himself in the Padishah's presence.

Baber crossed the Jumna and by forced riding arrived at Kanauj, only to find that the enemy had evacuated it in order to take up a position on the left bank of the Ganges. He made camp on the other side in full view of them, and set his engineers to work building a pontoon bridge for the passage of his troops.

The Afghàns opposite watched the work and laughed. The construction went on, covered by the fire of cannon and matchlock. Master Ali outdid himself on that day, firing as many as sixteen balls from each of his guns. Unfortunately, he lost his largest piece, his Big Fatimah, so to speak; he had loaded it rather heavily in order to silence a company of scoffers on a hill across the river, and it had burst.

The bridge was finished at last, and with it the laughter. On Friday, the thirteenth of March, the troops pushed across, drove the enemy back from the bridgehead and were in a fair way of winning the battle from them when orders came to retire to their camp at once!

It was a significant, if odd, consideration, that prevented the emperor from pushing on to a complete victory. For the Mussulman, whose day began at sunset, it was already Saturday. Now, he had begun his campaign this year, like the last, on the Persian New Year's Day. And he had won his greatest battle of the past year on a Saturday. To look for a victory again on the same day was asking too much of Fortune!

And so the troops were marched back across the bridge to their camp, to the vast relief of the rebels.

They made good use of the breathing spell; for when Sunday came Baber learned that the foes had fled.

Seven days later the imperial troops entered Lucknow and captured Bayazid's family; and the emperor threw a detachment after the man himself, who had galloped off to hide in the thorn-groves of the plain. A week later he camped near Oudh to set up the machinery of its government and to determine the amount of its assessable revenues. A few days later, the third of April, he hunted in the environs, which he was told were alive with game. It was Baber's belief that recreation is essential to clear-visioned statesmanship.

Once again there is a break in his journal, this time of five and a half months. When it is resumed, on the eighteenth of September, we find him giving audience in his cabinet at Agra.

The list of those he received is a curious *melange*: his son, Askari; the celebrated historian Khandamir; a poet who specialized in riddles; a performer upon the *kanun*, the Turkish zither.

The youngest in the audience that day was the most important. Although his son was only twelve years of age, Baber had called him in to talk with him about the affairs of Multan. It was another example of apparent precocity in the childern of high birth. As a matter of fact, Askari was being initiated, while adaptable, into the workings of army and state, just as a son of the people was early taught his father's trade. The problems of government cannot be solved by any abracadabra. Under Baber they were handled with common sense alone, as requiring no long technical apprenticeship such as is demanded in our finical old European states. The Turks possessed the instinct for sane government.*

Even then it was easier to be a politician than an emperor. But although he was far from having done with opposition, particularly among the insurgents in the east, Baber now appeared to be solidly planted on the imperial throne. The emperor was worthy of his empire. He performed his part with *eclat*, both as ruler and patron of the arts, at the same time never negglecting his interest in the affairs of Central Asia and Persia.

Having ordered a "Garden of the Lotus" to be set out at Dholpur, and a pleasure-pavilion raised in the middle of it, he went to inspect the work. If war was his business, gardens and their palaces were his hobby and diversion. The spot, he found, demanded a more balanced landscape. He invited the nobles and officers of the imperial palace to build their houses and lay out their gardens about his own.

Immediately another difficulty arose. The red granite boulder, previously mentioned, was not large enough, though immense, to permit of being hollowed out into the apartments that he wanted. He ordered it to be converted into a covered reservoir containing a gigantic octagonal cistern. And to hasten the work he doubled the number of stonecutters. At the time, he tells us, he had engaged in his various artistic enterprises one thousand four hundred and ninety-one men of the stone craft alone. His dreams were realized with a swiftness almost as magical as Aladdin's.

* See Appendix D.

At Sikri, dissatisfied with the execution of his orders, he punished several of his superintendents. At Gwalior he examined minutely the palaces and pagodas of the Hindu princes, perched on the abrupt hill three hundred feet above the town. Everything there was faced with exquisitely carved stone; and the copper domes were overlaid with goldleaf. But Baber had little liking for Indian architecture: in spite of its beauty of detail, it lacked symmetry, it seemed grotesque and flimsy; the rooms of the palaces were poorly lighted and not at all ventilated. He was astonished by the enormous size of the idols, and offended by their scandalous nudity. At his commands they were mutilated.

On the seventh day of November a violent attack of marsh-fever confined him to his library. There, for the recovery of his health, he wrote a poem in honour of the venerable Obaid Allah, formerly the spiritual director of his father. He promised himself that he would write at least ten couplets a day until he was well. On Saturday the twenty-second, he composed the last fifty-one, and once more healthy and active, ordered his men to hold themselves ready for departure.

Then followed the gala nights and days of feasting with which he dedicated his new palace at Agra. The ambassadors from the Shah of Persia, from the Khan of the Uzbeks, from the Indian Princes—everyone was there. Great screens of fragrant green herbs hung before the palace windows and transformed the hot wind into perfumed freshness. As was the custom the Sultans, the Khans, the Amirs and the nobles came before dinner to present their gifts to the emperor, spreading out before him precious objects in gold and silver. When the feast was done, the emperor in his turn distributed magnificent bounty: superb robes, exquisite jewels, and priceless arms. He did not forget the artillerymen who had distinguished themselves in his last campaign; nor did he overlook the engineers who had built the bridge over the Ganges. And with special thoughtfulness—for gratitude was no pale sentiment with him—he rewarded the faithful companions of his wanderings after the loss of Andijan, so many years ago.

Then there were fights of camels against elephants, and of rams against their own kind. Miniature cities were stormed and defended. Indian jugglers performed their strange antics, and dancers whirled through their most intricate figures. Followed a rain of copper and silver pieces, even of gold, upon the curious mob of people outside the palace gates, that they might have a part in the fete.

But Baber could not still his regretful longings for the provinces won in his earlier years. Kabul and Badakshan were far away, and the hazard of governing them was great. If he was to hold them at all, he must have better communications between them and Agra. So, he named a commission which was to oversee the construction of a nine-hundred-mile highway to Kabul. He himself fixed the unit of measurement, setting it down in verse form in order that his men might be able to remember it easily.* A milestone in the shape of a minaret eighteen feet high was to be

* His unit was 3,660 metres, about 12,000 feet.

erected every nine miles; and every eighteen miles there was to be a post-house, fully provisioned and furnished with excellent horses for the hard-riding couriers of the empire.

He sent detailed instructions to his sons, who were at the helm of the old provinces, with good paternal advice on their personal affairs. He reproved Humayun for his love of solitude:

"Often have you repeated in your letters, 'I long to be alone.' But to be alone is an evil thing for a ruler. Royalty is the most tyrannical of servitudes. If you wish to please me, forego your savage taste for solitude, and try to consult with your lords at least twice a day."

He criticized Humayun's spelling and his style: "Without being habitually bad, your spelling is not as correct as it should be. You are given to careless slips. Then through lack of experience you employ affected expressions the sense of which is often obscure. Try to write naturally; use simple and clear terms. Then what you write will come easier both for you and for those whom you address."

In a letter to Khoja Kelan, who was still his confidant, he renews all of his earlier recommendations. The disorder at Kabul is due to the fact that six or seven people are trying to have a finger in the government. Let his, Baber's wives and sisters come on to Agra at once. They are far too interested in public affairs; and women have no business to mix in such things. Let Baber's instructions be followed; then, if order does not result, if the treasury does not grow, if the farmers do not prosper, the fault will obviously lie with Baber's deputy there. The walls of the *enceinte*, he insists, should be repaired ; they need attention.

He runs on : look to the careful provisioning of the city. See that visiting ambassadors are supplied with their running expenses. Restore the great mosque and keep the public baths and caravanserais in good condition. Finish the palace within the citadel, and tell the architect to discuss his plans with an assistant who will be sent at once from the palace here at Agra. Above all, be sure to regulate the spillways of the Kabul reservoir wisely; to increase the supply of water to the Promenade and to the royal gardens. Proceed at once to the planting of more trees on that hill near Nazargah. Be sure to lay out the lawns symmetrically, and to have the flowers that border them chosen for their fragrance.

And then the homesick Baber admits his old friend into his innermost heart. The Hindustan business is nearly settled; when it shall have been definitely finished, he trusts that he will be able once again to see Kabul, to end this gnawing nostalgia ; yes, and to regale himself once more with real melons and grapes.

"Lately, you know, they served me with melons like those at home; I ate them in tears. Since I deprived myself of wine, that consoler in trouble, I am always aware of an immoderate desire for it : and I repine because of that too. Fortunately the Divine Grace each day puts the temptation farther away. Imitate me, Khoja Kelan ! Renounce the forbidden drink! After all, our drinking parties had their most powerful charm in the congenial spirits which they brought together... Let me suggest, dear friend, that if you have no other boon companions than Sher Ahmed and Haidar Kuli, it should not be difficult to break with the vice!"

When he wrote that, Baber was in the field again. He had kept himself minutely informed of the happenings beyond Ganges. The reports of his generals had led him to believe that he would not be needed there. Consequently, he had put Askari in command of the army of the east.

He himself went westward toward the long forest stretches of Rajputana, because the way was short, the people were infidel, and the country was rich. "Plunder in war for the Faith is as lawful to the Mussulmans as their mothers' milk," Muhammad of Ghor had once said. Excellent pillaging was essential; something to revive courage and enforce vows, and something to fatten the treasury that had been lean since he abandoned the special stamp-tax. The lion of the Hindus, Rana Sanga, being dead, his two sons were at each other's throats. Baber conferred with Bikermajit, the younger of them, giving him Shamsabad in exchange for Rantanpur, each gaining by the exchange.

He was at Dholpur inspecting the marble coursing of an unfinished palace there on the day that a messenger arrived with the news that the pretender, Mahmud Lodi, had invaded the provinces eastward and was being supported by all the Afghans.

Instantly Baber changed his plans and marched to the point of danger. He left on the second of February,

1529. Along the route, travelling without halt, now by horse, now by boat, in failing health, he began to feel the burden of his years. They seemed far more than two score and six to a man worn by the fatigues of the march and endless responsibilities. Even while *en route* he refused to overlook the details of a multitude of diverse affairs. He never spared himself.

He received and dispatched envoys. He kept his journal. He carried on a large correspondence with friends and vassals. He consulted with engineers and architects on the works at Agra and Dholpur. He selected presents for his son Humayun on the occasion of the birth of a child, and for his son Damran on that of his marriage. He sent them collections of his poetry, along with notes on a system of simplified chirography, *Baberi*, that he had just invented. He had a transcript of his Memoirs made for Khoja Kelan, who had asked for it. He prepared the format of an edition of his works. He even presided over a series of wrestling contests.

Finally, he reached Dugdugi on the Ganges, about fifty miles as the crow flies above its junction with the Jumna. There he met Askari, who had fallen back before the enemy. Baber ordered him henceforth to follow the river down on the left bank, while he himself took the right, and to camp opposite the imperial army every night.

Baber had his reasons for the plan. The enemy were divided into three corps . the first, under the pretender, was besieging Chunar on the Ganges to the south of Benares; the second, under Sher Khan, was stationed at Benares; and the third, under Biban and Bayazid, was marching north.

But the emperor's name was the roar of a tiger to his foes. Scarcely had he arrived at Allahabad when the Afghans lost courage and raised the siege of Chunar ; they also packed off and away from Benares. They were equally timid at Behar, and the new lord of terror had plenty of time there to arrange the administration to his profit. Another million was added to his revenues.

He went on. Benares and Ghazipur he occupied without lifting a hand. And when he encamped on the frontier of Bengal, to the south of the Ganges near its confluence with the Gogra, a huge number of Afghan chiefs tendered their submission.

From them he learned that Mahmud the Pretender had taken refuge with the army of the Bengali immediately across the river from the Turks. There had always been good feeling between Baber and the prince, Nasrat Shah ; but now the attitude of the Bengal neighbour appeared equivocal—unfriendly, if not actively hostile. The Shah had welcomed his rival, he had barred the way after him, and he had prevented the pursuit of the flying rebels.

"Setting, nevertheless, the policy of conciliation above all others," Baber suggested amicable terms ; the Shah paraded his army along the opposite shore and turned a deaf ear to suggestions of peace. At that the emperor, reinforced by twenty thousand fresh men, resolved to make his neighbour repent.

But between him and the destruction of the Bengali flowed two broad rivers, the Ganges and the Gogra. The operation would be long and difficult, for the enemy were in considerable number ; and even had

Baber had enough boats—and he had not—to force a passage directly under the fire of their unusually skilful gunners would have been bloody business. To encompass the enemy's defeat at no prohibitive cost demanded perfectly co-ordinated tactics.

Ali Kuli was ordered to station his pieces on an elevation between the two rivers and to concentrate his musket fire upon the Bengali camp on the east bank. Mustafa was to take up his position below the confluence of the streams and pour his shot into the enemy's flotilla which was moored there, and upon the flank of the enemy.

Four of the main divisions of the army, under Askari, already lay north of the Ganges. These were to cross the Gogra and divert the attention of the enemy while Baber's artillery was ferried over behind their backs. The fifth division was to support Ali, then cross under cover of his guns ; while the sixth was to concentrate about Mustafa's battery on the right bank of the Ganges.

The complex movement went off perfectly. In two days the fifth and sixth corps were over the larger river and were marching toward the Gogra, while Mustafa engaged the attention of the fleet. Two days later, news came that Askari and his divisions were ready on the other side of the Gogra.

On Thursday, the sixth of May, 1529, the battle began.

As Baber had planned, the Bangalis were inveigled into his son's trap. The instant their backs were turned the emperor ordered his last two divisions to cross the second river as best they could—swimming it when the boats and the rafts gave out. Once over they were to take the enemy in the rear.

This was done, brilliantly and in the face of determined resistance. Attacked in front, rear, and flank the enemy had no chance. Baber had created a victory out of apparently impossible materials. Once again he proved himself of the blood of Timur and Genghis Khan.

The Afghan lords fled like sparrows before the swoop of the hawk. The whimpering Nasrat sought peace, and was amazed to receive the same terms that Baber had offered him before the battle. Leniency was the better part of wisdom then, for the country would soon be lost under the steaming floods and mists of rainy season. And Lord Baber might rest now, content with the gain of all the Bengal lands between the Gandak and the Gogra that had formerly been held in fief by the Lodi.

At Lucknow, to the north-west, Biban and Bayazid were still in the field, but trembling on the verge of flight. The time was past when the emperor had need to fight in order to rout his enemies. The rumour of his approach, like the smoke of a jungle-fire, swept the country clean before him. The rebels fled pellmell to the south, the frontiers of Bundelkund, and beyond. In vain he tried to cut them off; terror freshened their horses, his own failed him through weariness... And the rains began to fall.

He wheeled about and flew back to Agra. The distance was a good one hundred and sixty miles. He left Adampur on Tuesday at mid-night and rode into his capital on Thursday at nine in the evening averaging eighty-five miles a day in that tropic downpour.

Apparently Nature herself wished to reward him for the extraordinary feat. For the next day, the twenty-fifth of June, he had the pleasure of enjoying some excellent melons and grapes, the first ever grown in India, which he had planted in his own "Garden of the Eight Paradises."

CHAPEER SIXTEEN

THE TRAGIC DEATH

MASTER now of all the domain that the Lodi had once ruled, master of an annual revenue of many millions, creator of an empire that stretched from the Himalayas to Gwalior and Chanderi and from the Oxus to Bengal, Baber might without presumption liken himself to the chief princes of the earth, to the Shah of Ispahan and the Sultan of Stamboul, and to the puissant and mysterious Lord of China.

Yet discontent gnawed at his heart. It arose not from his mighty and restless ambition driving him on to new exploits, but from a regret that his work was not completed. The very grandeur of his achievement made him more keenly aware of the goal at which he still aimed and which he still missed. So that when occasion drew him back to the road of his youtn, back to his charging horsemen, whom he had thought never to see again, he glowed with happiness.

India was a superb prize; but his desires, his honour and the blood of Timur, whispered the name "Samarkand." For his life Baber dared not break away from his realm at the moment. But his heart burned at thought of winning back the high hills of home, and its jewel of turquoise and gold. And then came news of the battle of Djam.

During the minority of Tahmasp, the king of Persia, the Uzbeks in Samarkand had grown insolent, thinking to profit by the weekness of that child. They had, in the years 525-28, snatched Merv, Meshed and Astrabad, and were on the point of besieging Herat when they were smitten into flight and silence by a powerful hand.

The hand was Tahmasp's, who was now come to the throne at the age of fourteen, revealing himself to the world as having the makings of a very great prince. He was a man already and a very grim one, black of skin, black of hair, black of humour, a man without laughter and preoccupied with the dreams that peopled his nights. He had lifted his head suddenly, gathered together forty thousand veterans of his father's following, and had cut the Uzbeks to pieces at Djam on September 26, 1528.

When Baber learned of the battle, he ordered his eldest son to ride back furiously to Badakshan, post of the advance-guard and place of honour in the empire. His instructions were to march at once upon Samarkand, Hissar or Herat as circumstances favoured.... "If you can occupy the first, make it your headquarters. It is hour home. Above all, no loitering, no laziness! For the poet Nizami has said :

Empire and languor are incompatible.
Hasten, and you can take the world in your grasp !"

Humayun marched upon Samarkand and occupied Hissar beyond the Amu, but he relaxed his vigilance when black Tahmasp withdrew from the east on his way to wrest Baghdad from the Osmanlis.

Here, in the middle of a note devoted to September 7, 1529, the Memoirs come brusquely to an end. The author had written his last word.

For the story of the last fifteen months of his life the sketchy character of the historical chronicles may be filled in fortunately by details from the writing of his cousin Muhammad Haidar and the Memoirs of his own daughter, Gul Badan.*

Although he had his eyes forever turned toward the place of his birth, even though he told Humayun and Khoja Kelan that he meant to return as soon as circumstances permitted, Baber left nothing undone that would make his work and his dynasty permanent in India. He called upon all of his relatives, Mongols as well as Turks, upon all the vassals of his father and of his ancestors, and upon all the princesses of his house, begging them to make India their home. He gave them money, houses, and lands. And as soon as peace was assured he ordered his harem down from Kabul, and sent for his sister Khansadeh and his best beloved Maham.

To her he had written a letter instructing her to leave Kabul at once : the journey would require five months, and she must be at his palace in Agra before the rainy season ; he would meet her at the town of Aligarh, sixty miles to the north of the capital, and escort her to his palace.

On the twenty-seventh of June the furious tempest and rain of the monsoon beat down over the country.

* A third source of importance is a fragment appended to the Baber Nameh, in Baber's name and written in the first person, but which appears to be one of the four additions that the Padishah Jahangir placed at the end of his great-grandfather's work, early in the following century.

On the same day through the mire of the northern road came a massenger to Lord Baber. Maham had travelled fast in her anxiety to see her lord at the appointed place. When he did not appear, she had ridden on alone to the capital, and was now only two leagues away, pressing close on the heals of the messenger who now spoke to her lord.

Baber did not wait for his horse but caught up his robes and ran through the storm and mud of the highway to meet her. When they encountered, she would have dismounted to greet him, but he would not hear of it; and accompanied her on foot for the rest of her journey.

Maham had with her the little Gul Badan, aged six, daughter of the emperor by another wife. The child, when presented to her father, threw herself at his feet, overwhelmed to find herself before this magnificent and glorious monarch. Tenderly and graciously he picked her up, asked her a hundred questions, and took her in his arms.

"And I," she says in her Memoirs, "tiny and insignificant, felt a happiness impossible to describe!"

Thus did Baber reveal once again the charming traits of his character—his spontaneity, his disdain for appearances, and his affectionate disposition; traits which we can appreciate more since the expression of intimate feeling was rare in men of his day.

The delicacy of his tact and his thoughtfulness became proverbial. It had been his custom every Friday to pay his respects to his aunts. Once, such a visit being due, it happened that an insufferably hot wind was blowing. Maham advised her husband not to venture out : he was ill, the weather was impossible. and his aunts would understand.

'My dear friend," he answered, "I wonder that you should suggest such a thing! The daughters of Sultan Abu Said Mirza have lost their father, their brothers, their husbands. Who is there to comfort them if I do not ?"

The incident had a sequel : it made him think that perhaps he had not given sufficient proof of his regard for the lonely women. He ordered his architects to refurnish and redecorate their houses precisely as they might wish.

His health began to fail.

Time had been when in the full of his tremendous strength he had caught up a man under each arm and run with them around the battlements of a fortress, leaping the embrasures. As late as March of 1529 he writes, "I have just swum the Ganges—for amusement. I had crossed by swimming every river I had met except this. I made it in thirty-three strokes. After a breath I swam back." He had known tremendous days, too, in the saddle, days when he had ridden eighty miles without rest and food. But a wandering, racking life with its periods of hard drinking and constant use of hashish, had eaten into his superb vitality. Sickness overtook him; Maham had been right in her warning.

Now he was subject to serious and repeated attacks of marsh-fever. He suffered from a chronic enteritis apparently acquired as a result of an attempted poisoning in the year 1526. At that time, shortly after the battle of Panipat, the mother of the dead Sultan

Ibrahim had given one of the palace cooks a toxic powder, which he had sprinkled over the emperor's food. Baber had been seriously ill for a long time afterwards.

In addition, he complained frequently in his Memoirs of certain ailments, that from his boyhood had kept him to his bed for days and weeks. His enormous physical vigour concealed, without doubt, a dangerous and obscure lesion.

And while his body drooped under a growing weakness, his disenchanted soul drooped as wearily under the gifts of destiny. His hands overflowed with the fruits of harvest ; but they were not the ones that hope had sown. The poets had from his earliest years taught him to distrust the good of this fugitive world. They had instructed him in the contemplation of the Absolute, and in mysticism that covered itself with the mantle of traditional creeds but that left the mind open and free.

More and more the princely philosopher felt within him an impatience with the noise of the players on the tawdry, smoky stage of this world ; he dreamed of composing himself somewhere in the clarity of the outer universe and listening to the eternal silence that here was broken by the interludes of human vanity, exacting its minute of applause.

They called him *Calender* the Mendicant Friar, for he who had fed on the glory of his century was indifferent to it ; he found it tasteless, so that desire for it troubled him no longer. This title accompanies his name on the inscription in his mosque at Oudh.

To his family he had confided that imperial power

was as ashes in his mouth, and that he wished to live henceforth as a dervish He dreamed of retiring to his gardens in Zerafshan, with a single ewer-bearer in the place of his thousand servants.

His adored Maham, and his children wept at the thought and used every argument to dissuade him. But what weighed most was this : he was above everything a true soldier, a true sportsman ; was not the man to quit post or game, at least until he had found a substitute.

Who could replace him ? His son Humayun was dear to him, he was brave ; but he was also thoughtless, reckless, and of an untrustworthy and eccentric temperament. In addition, he had just proved a great disappointment to his father in failing at Samarkand when every circumstance favoured him.

Baber's vizier, Khoja Nizam-ud-Din Ali Barlas, a friend of his and a very influential chief of the old Turkish party, then put forward Muhammad Mahdi Khoja, husband of Khansadeh, the Padishah's sister. . . . Khansadeh had always had the ear of her brother.

Jealous of her son's future, Maham advised him of this move. Humayun left precipitately his post at Badakshan, in the month of August, 1529, giving as a pretext his solicitude for the health of his father of which he said he had had bad news. He did not forewarn the emperor of his coming, nor did he take any pains to safeguard Badakshan in his absence. Leaving no one in control, he sped to Kabul. There he persuaded his ten-year-old brother, Hindal, to take his place. And without waiting to see if this were done, he hurried on down to Agra on his father's post-horses, to find him chatting with Maham.

Baber flared up into a towering rage. The mother tried to excuse her son, but the emperor considered his act as nothing short of desertion, rendered the more unpardonable because Badakshan was, as a consequence, temporarily without a ruler and defenceless against attack or uprising. Humayun was sequestered for a term in the small town of Sambhal, one hundred miles north of the capital.

The result of his rash conduct was soon apparent. When the nobles of Badakshan saw their lord ride so hastily away, they looked about them for a leader of mettle. Fearful of being attacked by the Uzbeks, they summoned the adventurous Said Khan, Mongol chief of Eastern Turkestan. He accepted the invitation with alacrity. But he arrived seventeen days after Hindal ; and the nobles, who had urged him to come, now refused their support. Angry at the trick, he laid siege to the royal castle and ravaged the surrounding country.

Baber the adventurer and knight-errant would have been plunged into war again. aber Bthe emperor merely gave out that he was going north to the mountains for a pleasure trip.

As far as Lahore he went, attended by the vast pomp and thunder of his thousand retainers and his impeccably trained army. His troops entered the city marching in excellent order beneath the red-and-yellow standards ; elephants, gold-caparisoned and sparkling with gems, led the imperial cortege, and behind came a host of servants clad in silks and brocades.

Said Khan understood. He raised his siege and retreated, protesting that he had had no other thought than the protection of Badakshan from Uzbek ravages.

Baber wisely took Said's speech with a grain of salt and remained at Lahore until the fourth of March, 1530. But when he had returned to Delhi for a two-month hunt and had led a punitive expedition against a lord of the Rajputani, the curtain of his life shook with the breath of his imminent passing.

The details of his death are scanty. We have only gossip, vague conventional tales. Their writers are too visibly concerned to clear Humayun's reputation. And they insist too anxiously that his relations with his father were adequately filial to the very end. The awkwardness, inaccuracy and inconsistency of their explanations show that they attempt to conceal a deplorable truth.

Gul Badan is the most exact and sincere, and she says enough to throw daylight upon the official embarrassment.

Apparently, Humayun remained six months in disgrace at Sambhal. While there he fell gravely ill, and was so long in recovering that his father "ended by permitting them to speak of him at court," according to Jahangir's report. The young prince was brought to Agra on a litter ; and his mother, fearing that his illness was mortal, threw herself at the feet of her husband : "You do not suffer, because you have many other subjects and many other sons. But I have only him, my one child."

According to the chronicles, Baber then reflected

that he had nothing in the world, save himself, more dear than the son of his well-beloved. He would offer himself as a ransom for the sick child, in the hope that God would accept the sacrifice.

He entered the room of the sick Humayun and walked three times around the bed, saying as he did so, "I take upon myself all that you are suffering." Immediately his son improved, and Baber's health declined. Shah Jehan, four generations later, had a miniature painted to confirm the story. It is probably pure invention ; but, true or false, it surprisingly represents God himself as the accomplice of the parricide.

For Baber was poisoned. Gul Badan explicitly says that that was the opinion of the physicians who waited upon the emperor at the last. One man stood to gain most by the deed ; one man had the means to perpetrate it in security—Humayun. So much gratuitous testimony in his favour marks him for suspicion. Need the innocence of a son be protested so loudly and so often ?

For two or three months Baber remains in his bed, which he was never to leave. Muhammad Mahdi is never absent from the palace, the centre of a busy intrigue, strutting insolently about and certain of his succession. Then Humayun returns again from Sambhal, where he went on his recovery. An anecdote related by the "Chronicle of the Afghan Sultans" sheds a sinister light on the relations between father and son.

On a day, sick to death, wasted white under the deep stain of his wars, heart and sinews cracking under the poison, the emperor lies asleep in a room of the palace. He stirs uneasily beneath the light coverlet of red silk, and he opens his eyes. A corner of the veil of fear passes over his face for an instant at sight of a man standing by his bed, motionless and alone.

"How long have you been here?"

"Ever since my lord ordered me to come, an hour ago."

"I do not remember having sent for you. . ."

"Did my lord fear me?"

Baber is silent, his distrust goes from him in a sigh of weariness. His eyelids fall slowly to hide the clear sad eyes that have looked too long into the heart of man. When he speaks, he masks his thoughts in dark words of strange counsel:

"If God accord the throne to you, do not kill your brothers, but watch them very closely. . . Now leave me, Humayun, my son."

He sinks back, and with a hand draws the cover nearer his throat—a hand that is bright with gems and translucent with the light of death. . . The crimson silk he clutches is the only spot of colour in that chamber of white marble. High up and unseen in a gallery behind grills of delicately wrought marble a faithful woman watches over her lord.

On a second day, he lies upon his cushion before a window, looking eagerly out over his gardens, as green and glorious amid the black plains of Agra as are the eyes of the tiger in the darkness of the forest. He listens for the last time to the water falling from a fountain of onyx exquisitely inlaid with malachite by a Greek slave two hundred years before, an artist who had been slain lest his dream of beauty should not remain matchless. Beauty and death. Man must leave one for the arms of the other. . . Will his son Hindal come in time? Kabul is far away. . . and Samarkand . . . and the cliffs of Farghana.

Mir Bardi Beg is announced. He comes from Hindal! When he enters, the emperor berates him faintly, speaking lightly at the very gates of his dissolution:

"Rascal! Your sister's marriage at Kabul and your own at Lahore have delayed the news of my son. Is he a big lad now? Is he happy? Will he . . . come?"

Mir Bardi shows him a robe that Hindal has sent.

"Come nearer. Show me. If only I might see Hindal himself."

But when the third day comes, Hindal is not there. It is near midday on the twenty-sixth of December: Muhammad Mahdi no longer plays peacock in the garden-palace, for Humayun of the cruel face and the ominous watch has been proclaimed successor. Nothing remains but for the emperor to make his great abdication.

On December the twenty-sixth, 1530, he holds his last audience. Against the white walls the myriad colours of robes show like garden flowers thrown upon a snowy bank. In their silks of honour the lords are ranged, silent and apart from the cushions where dies the Prince Zahir-ud-Din, whom his followers called the Panther, his foes, the Tiger. Maham the well-beloved watches near him, and Khansadeh, to whom he will listen but very little longer now. And Humayun stands once more beside his father. . .

The Lord Baber turns his face a last time toward Agra, beyond the shadows of the window. Pink and white it lies within the green of its grass and its fruit trees. And over it the great minar raises its fluted shaft to heaven . . . he waits . . . then . . . *La'illah il Allah . . . Wa Muhammad rasul Allah*, the lance-sharp cry comes quivering out of the sky.

It is the summons to midday prayers. With a whispering of silk the nobles prostrate themselves before God and their emperor. Lord Baber's eyes close. The words, " . . . the Good, the Generous . . . " come wearily to the ears of those nearest him. The man, the believer, meets his Maker.

His oft-expressed wish was obeyed; his body was taken to the city of his regret—Kabul. There he rests by the side of his favourite wife in one of the ten gardens made by him on the last but one of the fifteen terraces that climb the tower-crowned hillock facing the far-off snows of the Paghman. He rests near his cascading fountains, the fresh clear waters of which sang the ineluctable passing of the hours of his life, while its stones bore a stanza of his own composition:

Here Spring renews her flowers each day;
Here young girls stand ready to pour the wine.
Drink of the pleasures offered, Baber! Once drained,
The cup of life will return to your hand no more.

CHAPTER SEVENTEEN

THE EMPIRE DEATH COULD NOT END

BABER had profited by his little hour. He lived only forty-eight years. But within that span he had known a surprising variety of fortunes, from the lowest indignity to the highest glory. On no other basis than an illustrious name he had reared a house of state that has had few equals, that has proved against time its vital worth.

Though his son nearly lost everything, his grandson, Akbar, a superlatively great statesman, restored the work and finished it, uniting India into a coherent body and assuring it an unprecedented prosperity. For two centuries the house stood firm; in becoming its masters the English could do little more than change its official servants.

The interest attaching to the founder of such a structure is peculiarly increased in that we are able to create an exact image of the man and of his life. At least, he appears intelligible and natural—a rare circumstance in history.

Memoirs are ordinarily most unreliable source-books for the history of events; they are notably false, for the most part, and nearly always written for a purpose. But in this work of Baber's we cannot evade the impression of truth and frankness. He indulges in no heated accusations, no special pleading;

offers not a single apology, and takes no sides. No doubt his comments upon his adversaries should be discounted. But of himself he speaks with the utmost simplicity ; he makes light of none of his faults, none of his errors. In no part of his story, save where he speaks with pride of his birth, may one discover the face of the egoist. One seeks in vain for the subtle artifices of vanity or for artful attempts to take to himself the credit of events.

Throughout, the reader takes the place of the *valet de chambre*. We have heard that no man is a hero to his valet. True enough, but truer this: his essential heroism is above the head of the smug dependant who is his shadow. Valet Crispin believes that greatness consists in absense of faults. Seeing only the vices the weaknesses, the vacillations and the remorses of his master, he thinks that he can do equally well. He conceives of the great man only as "suspended in air, removed from our society," to paraphrase Pascal.

Now, no man was less that than Baber. He was interested in everything : as indefatigable in his pursuit of pleasures as in the labours of war and of government; as extraordinary for his physical energy as for the vitality of his spirit. Disliking to be chained to one spot, the annual feasts seldom found him twice in the same place. Since childhood his life had swung from warfare to the chase, from lonely scouting for a bare living to learning the resources and character of a conquerred state, from the building of mosques, palaces and caravanserais to the construction of aqueducts, reservoirs and watered gardens. And if his chief joy lay in planting trees and in growing fruits, this charming weakness did not prevent him from conquering and governing an unruly world.

Love of action was one of the chief factors in his success. When he failed, he began over again, never tiring, yet rarely stubborn at the wrong moment. He seemed to move forward at random, yet what he lost here, he could win back there. A shrewd observer of life, he accumulated a treasure of experience that he used to his profit.

One observation by which he was guided was that Fate is the willing ally of great men—men with the will to be great. In no instance did he ever attribute a victory to his profound strategy or to his personal courage ; he rendered thanks to God and to Fate. For he knew that while wise preparation and ably concerted movements are the prerequisites of victory, they are not always the determining factor. Something always escapes prevision : a second of time, a mere nothing destroys the balance ; then luck takes charge, and the measure that carries the day is often contrary to human wisdom and to all the rules of the game.

Man is not strong enough to create events. It is Fortune that does this, and deploys them. But the man who is most watchful, most ready, siezes her as she flies and stays her. Baber had the genius of audacity, with the keen eye and quick mind that care little for prejudices, customs or opinions.

Like men of greater genius, Caesar and Napoleon he was superstitious. It was not a serious handicap. for he was the first to laugh at it. But in moments of doubt it gave direction to his actions. As for disquieting presages, evil omens, he usually ignored them. The auguries to which he paid attention were those which seconded his healthful spirit of optimism. They were evoked by that powerful dream tirring forever in his brain, the spring of his actions, the guide and tyrant of his will. The dream never gave him repose, lest it should not be realised. And it communicated to his desire for conquest a character of imperious necessity.

Perhaps the master-faculty of the man was his art of winning the hearts of his soldiers and of those who served him. He was graced with singular charm of person that still shines from his confidences, fresh and lively in spite of time and distance. We see him, liberal, prodigal of his favours, generous to a fault, impulsive and affectionate. He loved his friends so dearly that once, at the death of one of them, he remained disconsolate for days. Proud of them, he boasted of their virtues, spoke often of their invaluable services, and gave them the glory for his victories. Unaffected himself, he adroitly allied a graceful ease with the required formality. His high-spirited humour carried him through his worst misfortunes and joked about all things save two—military orders and solidarity between companions in arms. Nothing less could have controlled those turbulent, intractable folk, always ready for uprising or desertion. Truculence would have been impossible to the kindness of Baber's heart and the clarity of his mind. Tyranny he disdained as childish. Friends and beauty he loved, and to them gave his soul.

He had the flexible energy of the true commander; but it was the flexibility of steel. He came to scorn the help of unwilling folk, pardoned freely those who had offended, and extended his indulgence to those faithful ones who needed it. He could never be reproached with the magnificently horrible and useless atrocities of Timur and Genghis Khan; yet he did not hesitate to use sternness when it was needed. And occasionally he gave way to violent displays of anger and cruelty.

For he was temperate in nothing. He flung himself headlong into his pleasures. From his twenty-eight until his forty-fourth year he drank wine without *interruption; he found a way to get drunk without* discomfort four times in twenty-four hours. That habit he finally gave up, but he continued to take hashish. Yet even his intemperance, of which he speaks with such complaisance and in as much detail as if he were describing a battle, was in the main only a pretext for gathering around him his dearest friends so that they might talk and recite verses, sing and make music together—the means of securing an escape from formality and cares of state.

For the man's culture was broad and exceptionally refined. To the vigour and hardihood of his Turkish and Mongol ancestors he had added the breeding and knowledge of the Persians. He was a fencer of considerable prestige, an archer of note, and an excellent referee in all the sports of his day. On his horse he accomplished feats that were astounding for their speed and endurance. He crossed rivers by swimming them. At the same time he was a musician, both performer and composer; he was caligraphist, theologian, essayist, poet. He was master equally of the

Persian and the Turkish tongues. His Memoirs, richer and more varied in substance, sustain comparison with the *Anabasis* in point of formal composition. His poetry is not that of an amateur; he knew all the resources and tricks of the art—infinitely more complicated in the languages of the Orient than in ours. A subtle and nice critic, he was versed in the most intricate subtleties of metre and of grammar.

It is fascinating to watch him combine and alternate his various occupations. His Memoirs he writes in his tent, in the face of the enemy; his verses he composes in the field, while hunting, at the council. When by some chance he is kept to his library for a day, he makes note of its treasures. His literary works are no more an obstacle to his military and state affairs than are his pleasure parties. They fill the inevitable intervals of delay and inaction that are so difficult for an active man to endure. An old servant reports that he was never more active than when he was doing nothing. Baber's poetry is an integral part of his personality, an ingredient of his intellectual and moral vigour, without which he could never have exercised over others the spiritual domination that leads to empire.

No man was less imprisoned than this conqueror within the narrow limits of the actual. Prepared to accomplish the task for which he believed himself born, careful to fill his post honourably, what he loved was to meditate upon the insignificant thing that glory *is*, to contemplate its derisive inconstancy from the heights of mysticism and disillusionment. Without question, he would have renounced his perishable grandeur within his lifetime had he been able to find trusty hands into which to place it. "Say not," he wrote, "that the road is long from monarch to dervish; a monarch, I should be proud to serve dervishes."

He justified the magnificent epitaph written for him by his great-grandson, Jahangir :

"He marched to Conquest as to the Light, his face turned towards the world of spirits."

APPENDIX A

(*See p.* 61)

THE INTERVENTION OF OBAID ALLAH

AT this point the various copies of the *Baber Nameh* present a hiatus of more than one year, of which the reader is given no explicit warning. The royal historian tells how after his marvellous deliverance Baber rallied about him his faithful adherents, to the number of three hundred. Then he adds immediately that he determined to leave Farghana and seek his fortune elsewhere. Between these two sentences occurs a lapse of eighteen months, from December 1502 to June 1504.

This manner of placing the interruption in Baber's Memoirs resolves most of the difficulties that have been raised —particularly by Mrs. Beveridge in the notes to her translation — concerning the authenticity of the pages which tells of the prince's deliverance. The Persian edition halts abruptly in the middle of a sentence, at the moment when the young prince retires to say his prayers, but the best Turkish manuscript, that of Haidarabad, recounts the entire story. The style of it is perfectly consistent with that of the rest. And a number of details find partial confirmation elsewhere.

The two lords who came to Baber's rescue appear to have been Kutluk Barlas and Babai Beshaghir (Pergueri is a copyist's error) and are mentioned in other passages of the *Nameh*. Further, it is correct to count five stages *en route* from Kernan to Andijan. The distance by road is ninety-three miles, so that the stages would average about nineteen miles apart ; the obvious delay was undoubtedly due to the fact that the fugitives had to take by-roads. Finally, the incident of Obaid Allah and the dreams recorded are no more curious than many others which Baber relates without believing half of them. It is merely his way of shedding light on the strange turns of his fate.

True enough, the story in question here does contradict an anterior passage, where one finds the Mongol Khans—terrified at the news that Shaibani has promised Tanbal to intervene—raising the siege of Andijan, retreating by way of

Khojent and crossing the Syr River there, going apparently to Tashkent. That must have occurred just before Baber's flight ; so that he could not have taken refuge in Andijan at the time.

But under the circumstances such an action on the part of the Khans would have been inexplicable. It was at the end of October or the beginning of November. Shaibani could not at that late season have undertaken an expedition of any proportions at all. He did nothing of any import, in fact, during the year 1502. The text does not accommodate itself to the implied movements of the Khans, nor do the events that follow fit into the design.

One of two things must be admitted : either that the Mongols went into winter quarters on the right bank of the river—in which case they would have found the country bare, too poor to support as numerous an army as theirs ; or they returned to Tashkent, to recommence the campaign in the spring of 1503—an hypothesis that is supported by no passage in any of the historians.

It is therefore likely that the passage concerned here (Pavet de Courteille's translation, Vol. I, page 240) is a fragment dealing with the following year, the rest having been lost. It was poorly placed at the time of the collation of the multilated manuscript ; not knowing what to do, the Indian scribes inserted it after the affairs of the year 1502. Then, in order to make it agree with the preceding details about the Mongols at Andijan, they substituted "raised the siege of Andijan" for the expression "left Andijan," which apparently was in the original.

If this explanation is accepted, the events then become logical and coherent. By the time that their nephew fled from Akhsai the Khans had occupied Andijan, of which they had an imperative need and which was far too weak to beat off their attack. And there Baber spent the winter. In the spring of 1503 Shaibani took the field with superior forces ; the Khans, feeling themselves at a disadvantage among a hostile people, descended in haste to Khojent with the intention of going on to Tashkent. Plenty of details, too tedious to set down here, confirm this interpretation of events ; none disagree with it.

APPENDIX B

(*See pp.* 106, 134, 141)

THE MUHAMMADAN SECTS

THE Muhammadans are divided into two principal sects: the Sunnites, by far the more numerous, and the Shiites, found little outside of Persia. They have as their chief difference the question of the Prophet's succession.

1. The Sunnites consider that the first three Kalifs elected by the faithful were the legitimate heirs of the Envoy of God and as such are the spiritual and temporal chiefs of Islam. These three were Abu-Bekr, Omar, and Othman. After them came Ali Hassan and the Omayyaiads and Abbassids, the succession failing when the last of them, a refugee in Egypt, conferred his rights upon the Ottoman Sultan Selim I in 1517.

2. The Shiites, on the contrary, consider the first three Kalifs nothing but accursed usurpers. For them Ali alone had the right to follow Muhammad: first, because he was the cousin and nearest relative of the Founder ; second, because he married the only surviving daughter of the Prophet ; and third, because (according to tradition) Muhammad during his lifetime designated him as his heir.

This latter sect gave to the chief of Islam the title *Imam* (Director) rather than Kalif. For them, the office is not to be acquired by human appointment but rather is God-given. When Ali died, the dignity of *Imam* passed to his legitimate heirs from father to son. There were only twelve *Imams* in all, the last of them dying without issue in 870.

The devout among the Shiites of Baber's time frightened simple souls by their fanaticism. They scandalized them by their singular opinions and horrified them by their nocturnal rites. For the good of their souls they killed all whom they met. They believed in a spiritual world but denied the resurrection of the dead ; they believed that from time to time God manifested himself in human form ; as, for example, in the body of Ali, who after his death regained his own identity in Heaven. And they had the supreme perversity to maintain that the laws of the Koran had been valuable only to the contemporaries of the Prophet, and that now Reason alone was the proper guide.

3. The Ismailites, a third sect, are Shiites who recognize Ismail as the seventh Imam rather than Mussa, his younger brother.

APPENDIX C

(*See p.* 186)

THE ARMIES OF CONQUERORS

It is largely because of human nature's delight in superlatives, that the world's famous captains have always been given perfectly fabulous hosts. Great generals must have huge armies. The names of Genghis Khan, Timur, Alexander and Xerxes mount like wine to the brain of the historian. His figures become figures of speech : "one hundred thousand" becomes his minimum. He soon leaps to "one million". He does this with a sense of relish, but also because he knows that his reader will tremble with pleasurable awe at the passing of a conqueror who leads countless warriors.

Whenever it has been possible to check the army lists, we are surprised at the small number of men engaged even in the most important battles and campaigns of the world. The expedition into Kashgar led by the Mongol, Said Khan, Baber's cousin, was considered one of the principal military events of his time. It was preceded by a methodical census of the troops that took part in it. Muhammad Haidar, who was present and had the rolls under his eyes, informs us that the number was four thousand seven hundred men, exclusive of rearguard.

At no time had Genghis Khan himself an army of more than one hundred thousand men. Subutai, the commanding general of his successor, overthrew all the armies that Europe sent against him and penetrated as far as Vienna—with twenty-five thousand men. And when he withdrew, it was not for military reasons but simply because the death of the Khan demanded his returnto Mongolia.

And we have serious grounds for believing that the legendary multitudes that invaded Greece under Xerxes were of the same order of grandeur. When one examines the narrative of Herodotus in this light, one is forced to admit that the Father of History is engaged in passing a camel through the eye of a needle.

APPENDIX D

(*See p.* 212)

THE TURKS AS RULERS

FEW facts in history are more remarkable than the aptitude which the Turks and their cousins the Mongols and the Manchus displayed for the exercise of authority and governmental functions. They have held with equal vigour the sceptres of the Sons of Heaven, the King of Kings, and of Caesar Augustus. Their military superiority and their natural respect for order do not suffice to explain the fact. To tell the truth, they never troubled themselves over administrative detail, leaving it to the native underlings; but they had the faculty of command, of exacting obedience without fuss, from people of every rank and race. Their simple good sense foresaw and resolved difficulties; their absence of prejudice and of factional spirit preserved them from breaking their heads on obstacles. They were true democrats, giving every man of ability a chance. They were never excelled in government until the rise of modern Europe. During the two centuries that preceded Timur, Hindustan enjoyed one hundred and eighty years of peace and order.

Their reputation has suffered, but that is because of the fact that those among them who became Mussulmans had to govern, in Turkey and India, people of different religions. These, by reason of their religious hatred, were led to create astonishing tales of the tyranny and cruelty of their lords.

BIBLIOGRAPHY

The principal source of our knowledge is the *Baber Nameh*, the Memoirs written by Baber himself in eastern, or Jagatai, Turkish. The original manuscript has disappeared. We possess a single ancient copy, called the Elphinstone manuscript, dating from about 1560. It is good but very incomplete. Haidarabad possesses the best of the later copies, which, judging from the paper used, was written about 1700. Unknown for a long time, it was finally published and edited by Mrs. A. S. Beveridge, and is to be found in the E. J. W. Gibb collection, London, 1905. In 1714 a Russian mission acquired another manuscript, called the Bokhara manuscript, derived principally from the Persian translation of the Turkish. Kehr published a careful, edition of it in London, 1737, which Ilminsky had printed at Kazan in 1857. This text, though imperfect, is very useful because it contains details not to be found elsewhere.

In 1589, Abu-ur-Rahim, at the command of the emperor Akbar, translated Baber's work into Persian under the title *Waki' at-i-Baberi*. It is a good translation, corresponding exactly with the Turkish manuscript of Haidarabad. In 1826 Leyden and Erskine published an English version of this in London.

Since then two other translations of the Memoirs have been brought out in Europe : in French by Pavet de Courteille from the Ilminsky text (Paris, 1871, 2 volumes); and in English by Mrs. A. S. Beveridge, based on the Haidarabad manuscript (London, 1921, 2 volumes). This latter translation is accompanied by numerous and important notes.

Sir Denison Ross published a collection of the poems (divan) of Baber in 1910.

Other sources :

ORIENTAL

Mirza Mohammed Haidar, Baber's cousin: *Tarikh-i-Rashidi*, translated into English by E. Denison Ross, with a preface by N. Elias. London, 1895.

Gul Badan, Baber's daughter: *Humayun Nameh*, translated into English by Mrs. A. S. Beveridge, London, 1902.

Khandamir. *Habib-us-siyar* (Part IV, The Life of Ismail Safavi). Teheran, 1271 Heg.

Id. Life of Sultan Hussayn Baikara, translated by H. Ferte. Paris.

Muhammad Salih. *Shaibani Nameh*, a Turkish poem edited and translated into the German by Vamberg. Vienna, 1885. Re-edited by Melioransky and Samoilovitch. St. Petersburg, 1908.

Mir Sikander. *Tarikhi Alam Aral* (Shah Abbas)—valuable for its details of Baber's third occupation of Samarkand.

Sayid Jamal. *Arghun Nameh.*

Mir Maasun. *Tarikhi Sind.*

Ahmed Yadgar. *Tarikhi Salatini Afghana* (the Lodi dynasty). Yahia ibn Abd-ul-Latif *Lub-ul-tawarikh.*

Nizam-ud-Din Ahmed. *Tabakatai Akbari.*

Badauni. *Muntakhab-ul-tawarikh.*

Abd-ul-Fazl Allami. *Akbar Nameh.*

Ferishta, *Tarikh*, translated by J. Briggs (History of the Rise of the Mahomedan Power in India till A.D. 1612). London, 1829.

Khafi Khan. *Muntakhab-ul-Lubab.*

Subhan Rai. *Khulasat-ul-tawarikh*, translated by Gilchrist.

The most interesting extracts from the native chronicles have been translated in *The History of India, As Told by Its Own Historians*. Elliot and Dowson. London, 1867-77, 8 vols.

EUROPEAN

W. Erskine. *History of India. Baber and Humayun.* London, 1854. The first volume contains the most complete biography of Baber.

Stanley Lane-Poole. *History of the Moghul Emperors*. London, 1892.

Id. Baber. Oxford, 1899.

R. Williams. *An Empire Builder—Baber*. London, 1918.

Vincent Smith. *The Oxford History of India*. Oxford, 1919.

Malcolm. *Histoire de la Perse*. Paris, 1821.

Howorth. *History of the Mongols*. London, 1876-88, 4 vols.

Oaten. *European Travellers in India*. London, 1909.

F. G. Browne. *A History of Persian Literature*. Cambridge, 1920-24, 2 vols.

Ishwari Prasad. *History of Medieval India*. Allahabad, 1928.

The Cambridge History of India.

L. Bouvat. L'Empire Mongol, Vol. VIII of the *Histoire du Monde*. Cavaignac. Paris, 1927.

INDEX